PRACTICE
MAKES
PERFECT™

English
Verb Tenses
Up Close

Mark Lester

**Mc
Graw
Hill**

New York   Chicago   San Francisco   Lisbon   London   Madrid   Mexico City
Milan   New Delhi   San Juan   Seoul   Singapore   Sydney   Toronto

The *McGraw-Hill* Companies

1 2 3 4 5 6 7 8 9 10 11 12 13 14 15 16   QFR/QFR   1 9 8 7 6 5 4 3 2

ISBN   978-0-07-175212-1
MHID   0-07-175212-9

e-ISBN 978-0-07-175354-8
e-MHID   0-07-175354-0

Library of Congress Control Number 2011922820

McGraw-Hill, the McGraw-Hill Publishing logo, Practice Makes Perfect, and related trade
dress are trademarks or registered trademarks of The McGraw-Hill Companies and/
or its affiliates in the United States and other countries and may not be used without
written permission. All other trademarks are the property of their respective owners.
The McGraw-Hill Companies is not associated with any product or vendor mentioned in
this book.

McGraw-Hill products are available at special quantity discounts to use as premiums
and sales promotions or for use in corporate training programs. To contact a
representative, please e-mail us at bulksales@mcgraw-hill.com.

This book is printed on acid-free paper.

Contents

Preface

This book is a user's manual for English verb tenses. Three chapters introduce (1) stative and dynamic verbs, (2) perfect tenses, and (3) progressive tenses. Ten other chapters cover the 10 tenses of English. Each of these specific tense chapters begins with a survey of the different meanings and uses of the tense, followed by an in-depth examination of each, paying particular attention to topics that are most likely to be troublesome to nonnative speakers, including how that tense is like and unlike other tenses that have similar meanings.

Because the book is focused exclusively on verb tenses, it is able to go into much greater depth than other books intended for nonnative speakers. A particular focus of this book is on lower-frequency meanings and uses that are generally ignored in most books. For example, the discussion of the present tense identifies no fewer than seven different uses, three of which are for present time, two for past time, and two for future time. Most books discuss only one or two of these meanings.

Another example is in the treatment of the three progressive tenses. For some reason, the progressive tenses have a number of rather idiomatic uses that are rarely mentioned in most ESL books. Because most of these idiomatic uses occur in casual conversation rather than in formal writing, most advanced nonnative speakers are unaware that these uses even exist even though they are actually fairly common in conversation and often convey significant information, attitudes, and social commentaries.

How to use this book

Each chapter is designed to stand alone. If a particular verb tense is a problem for you, you can read the relevant chapter without any prerequisite with one major exception: you *should* read Chapter 1, "Introduction to stative and dynamic verbs." So many problems with verb tenses are rooted in users' not recognizing stative verbs that it seems most efficient to have a single detailed treatment of stative and dynamic verbs that can be referred to when needed rather than have a bare-bones treatment in every chapter.

The other brief chapter introductions to the families of perfect and progressive verbs (Chapters 5 and 9, respectively) might be helpful but do not need to be read if you're comfortable with the concepts. Even so, Chapters 1, 5, and 9 do have exercises to hammer home knowledge.

Any example sentence marked with **X** is incorrect English. Those sentences marked with **?** indicate questionable or not fully presentable English.

All exercises in this book are covered in the Answer key.

Introduction to stative and dynamic verbs

Not all verbs are equal when it comes to the meaning and use of verb tenses. Verbs can be divided into two families or classes: **stative** and **dynamic**. These classes very much affect our choices of which verb tense to use. As the names imply, **stative** verbs refer to ongoing, existing states or conditions that are not time bound. **Dynamic** verbs, on the other hand, refer to actions or activities that take place in a moment or limited period of time and then are completed. Dynamic verbs are time bound. For example, compare the meanings of the stative verb *own* and the dynamic verb *wash*:

Stative	Roberta <u>owns</u> a pickup truck.
Dynamic	Roberta <u>is washing</u> her truck.

The stative verb *owns* implies that Roberta's ownership of the truck is an ongoing, existing state: she has owned the truck for some time, she owns the truck now, and she will continue to own the truck for some indefinite time into the future. Her ownership of the truck is not a time-bound activity (even though, obviously, it does not last forever).

The dynamic verb *wash* is quite different: the act of washing something is necessarily a temporary, time-limited activity. Roberta started washing her truck a few minutes ago, and in a few minutes, she will have finished the act of washing her truck. Washing a truck is a time-bound activity.

Notice that the stative verb example is in the present tense. The basic meaning of the present tense is "state that has existed in the past, exists now, and will continue to exist into foreseeable future," a meaning that is quite compatible with the inherent meaning of stative verbs. However, the present tense is not compatible with the "temporary, time-limited activity" meaning of dynamic verbs. Accordingly, we cannot use the dynamic verb *wash* in the bare present tense without other qualifiers:

X Roberta <u>washes</u> her truck.

We can make stative verbs grammatical in the present tense by adding an adverb of frequency; for example:

Roberta <u>washes</u> her truck *every weekend*.

The addition of the adverb of frequency *every weekend* changes the meaning of the sentence by now making the action of the verb habitual or cyclical. Actions that are habitual or cyclical are reoccurring and are not time bound, thereby making the action of the verb compatible with the ongoing nature of the present tense. But without the added adverb of frequency, the use of present tense by itself is ungrammatical.

The dynamic verb *wash* can be used in any progressive tense because the basic meaning of the progressive tenses (action carried out in a particular moment of time) is perfectly suited for the time-limited action of dynamic verbs:

Present progressive	Roberta <u>is washing</u> her truck now.
Past progressive	Roberta <u>was washing</u> her truck when you called.
Future progressive	Roberta <u>will be washing</u> her truck this afternoon.

However, if we attempt to use the stative verb *own* in any progressive tense, the result is predictably ungrammatical:

Present progressive	**X** Roberta <u>is owning</u> a pickup truck.
Past progressive	**X** Roberta <u>was owning</u> a pickup truck at the time.
Future progressive	**X** Roberta <u>will be owning</u> a pickup truck when she moves to Alaska.

Note: in Chapter 10, "The present progressive tense," there is a much more detailed discussion of why nonnative speakers make so many errors by using stative verbs with the present progressive tense.

Some verbs can be used either as dynamic verbs or as stative verbs. When this happens, the two different uses of the same verb will necessarily have different meanings. Here is an example with the verb *weigh*:

Stative	The steak *weighs* a pound.

In this example, the stative verb *weigh* describes an ongoing condition, namely that the steak weighs a pound. The sentence is a factual statement not bound by time: the steak will continue to weigh a pound for the foreseeable future.

Dynamic	The butcher *is weighing* the steak right now.

In this example, the dynamic verb *weigh* expresses an action carried out at a particular moment of time, an action that is definitely time bound: the butcher started weighing the steak a few moments ago, and in a moment or two, the butcher will be finished with the action of weighing.

As we would expect, the stative verb *weigh* cannot be used in any progressive tense:

Present progressive	**X** The steak is weighing a pound.
Past progressive	**X** The steak was weighing a pound.
Future progressive	**X** The steak will be weighing a pound.

Here is a second example: *see*. The basic meaning of the verb *see* is "perceive," either physically with one's eyes or more abstractly, as in to "know" or "figure out." In both of these meanings, *see* is a stative verb:

Physically

Present tense	I see you.
Present progressive tense	**X** I am seeing you.

Abstractly

Present tense	I see what you mean.
Present progressive tense	**X** I am seeing what you mean.

However, there is a third, quite idiomatic meaning of *see*: "be romantically involved with someone." In this meaning, *see* is a dynamic verb:

Present tense	**X** Harriet sees a young man from her school.
Present progressive tense	Harriet is seeing a young man from her school.

Before we get into the details of how to identify stative verbs, see if you can distinguish stative and dynamic verbs in the following exercise just based on your intuitive sense of the fit between the meaning of these particular verbs and the present and present progressive tenses. If the meaning of the verb fits with the timeless, ongoing nature of the present tense, then you can reasonably guess that it is a stative verb. If the verb fits with the temporary, time-bound meaning of the present progressive tense, then you can reasonably guess that it is a dynamic verb.

*Rewrite the following sentences replacing the underlined base-form verbs with both the present tense and the present progressive tense forms. Compare both forms, and decide which one seems intuitively correct. If the present tense sentence seems correct and the present progressive seems wrong, label the verb "Stative." Conversely, if the present progressive tense seems correct and the present tense seems wrong, label the verb "Dynamic." The first two are done as examples, with "**X**" indicating incorrect English and "OK" identifying a correct sentence.*

Look. It <u>rain</u>.

PRESENT TENSE: Look. It <u>rains</u>.   **X**

PRESENT PROGRESSIVE TENSE: Look. It <u>is raining</u>.   OK

Rain is a dynamic verb.

Aunt Jane <u>like</u> her coffee with cream.

PRESENT TENSE: Aunt Jane <u>likes</u> her coffee with cream.   OK

PRESENT PROGRESSIVE TENSE: Aunt Jane <u>is liking</u> her coffee with cream.   **X**

Like is a stative verb.

1. I <u>count</u> to 10.

   Present tense: _____

   Present progressive tense: _____

   _____

2. He <u>hate</u> having to repeat himself.

   Present tense: _____

   Present progressive tense: _____

   _____

3. We all <u>hear</u> what we want to hear.

   Present tense: _____

   Present progressive tense: _____

   _____

4. We <u>want</u> to leave after work as soon as we can.

   Present tense: _____

   Present progressive tense: _____

   _____

5. The company <u>expand</u> its product line.

   Present tense: _____

   Present progressive tense: _____

   _____

6. I <u>make</u> a reservation for our trip next week.

   Present tense: _____

   Present progressive tense: _____

   _____

7. Their stock portfolio <u>consist</u> largely of bonds and conservative stocks.

   Present tense: _____

   Present progressive tense: _____

   _____

8. The publisher <u>review</u> her latest book.

   Present tense: _____

   Present progressive tense: _____

   _____

9. John <u>accept</u> that he is going to have to relocate.

   Present tense: _____

   Present progressive tense: _____

   _____

10. I <u>know</u> the answer.

    Present tense: _____

    Present progressive tense: _____

    _____

Because stative verbs pose such a problem for nonnative speakers, it is important to be able to identify stative verbs when you encounter them. There are far too many stative verbs (somewhere between 100 and 200) to just memorize a list. There is also the problem that many stative verbs can also be used as dynamic verbs (with different meanings, of course), so the fact that a given verb is on the list of stative verbs does not always mean that it is being used as a stative verb in any particular sentence.

Nearly all stative verbs fall into the following five semantic categories:

Category 1: Cognition and emotion (the largest category)
Category 2: Obligation, necessity, and desire
Category 3: Ownership and possession
Category 4: Measurement
Category 5: Linking verbs with the meaning of appearance and sense perception
(The term *linking verb* is explained in detail later.)

Here are some typical verbs in the five categories along with paired examples of the same verb used in the present tense and a progressive tense. The fact that the sentences are ungrammatical in the progressive tenses confirms that the verb is indeed a stative verb.

Category 1: Cognition and emotion
Examples: believe, doubt, hate, love, mean, think, understand

Present tense	I <u>understand</u> what you mean.
Progressive tense	**X** I <u>am understanding</u> what you mean.
Present tense	Sally <u>loves</u> being able to walk to work.
Progressive tense	**X** Sally <u>is loving</u> being able to walk to work.

Category 2: Obligation, necessity, and desire
Examples: desire, have to, need, prefer, promise, require, want, wish

Present tense	We <u>have to</u> find out what is going on.
Progressive tense	**X** We <u>are having to</u> find out what is going on.
Present tense	I <u>wish</u> I didn't have to get to work so early.
Progressive tense	**X** I <u>am wishing</u> I didn't have to get to work so early.

Category 3: Ownership and possession
Examples: belong, have, own, possess

Present tense	They <u>have</u> a small apartment near the university.
Progressive tense	**X** They <u>are having</u> a small apartment near the university.
Present tense	That dog <u>belongs</u> to our next-door neighbor.
Progressive tense	**X** That dog <u>is belonging</u> to our next-door neighbor.

Category 4: Measurement
Examples: consist of, contain, cost, equal

Present tense	Chain-saw fuel <u>consists of</u> a mixture of gas and oil.
Progressive tense	**X** Chain-saw fuel <u>is consisting of</u> a mixture of gas and oil.
Present tense	Two plus two <u>equals</u> four.
Progressive tense	**X** Two plus two <u>is equaling</u> four.

Category 5: Linking verbs with the meaning of appearance and sense perception

Examples: appear, be, feel, hear, look, seem, taste

Present tense	The left lane <u>appears</u> to be blocked.
Present progressive tense	**X** The left lane <u>is appearing</u> to be blocked.
Present tense	The children <u>seem</u> upset.
Present progressive tense	**X** The children <u>are seeming</u> upset.

EXERCISE

1·2

The underlined verbs in the following sentences are all stative verbs correctly used in the present tense. Decide which of the following five categories is the best fit for describing each of these stative verbs:

Category 1: Cognition and emotion
Category 2: Obligation, necessity, and desire
Category 3: Ownership and possession
Category 4: Measurement
Category 5: Linking verbs with the meaning of appearance and sense perception.
The first sentence is done as an example.

Your purchase <u>includes</u> a 30-day money-back guarantee.

ANSWER: Category 3: Ownership and possession

1. I <u>doubt</u> that we can afford to buy a new car right now.

   _____

2. The soup <u>tastes</u> way too salty.

   _____

3. My new car <u>has</u> a state-of-the-art GPS.

   _____

4. The decline in real estate values <u>amounts to</u> billions of dollars.

   _____

5. The new law <u>requires</u> all drivers to have proof of insurance.

_____

6. The noise <u>sounds</u> like it is coming from outside.

_____

7. Relatively few foreign students <u>belong to</u> fraternities or sororities.

_____

8. The kids <u>seem</u> cranky this morning.

_____

9. A new suit <u>costs</u> at least 200 dollars these days.

_____

10. His sudden change of policy <u>satisfies</u> no one.

_____

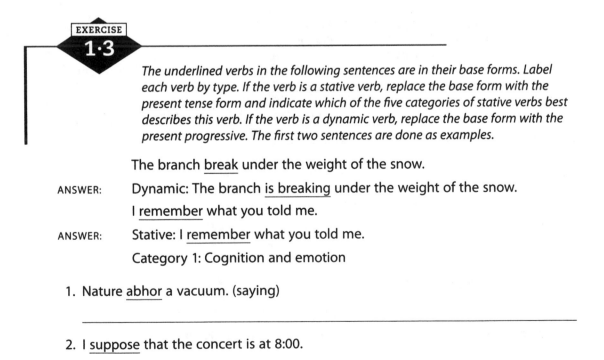

The underlined verbs in the following sentences are in their base forms. Label each verb by type. If the verb is a stative verb, replace the base form with the present tense form and indicate which of the five categories of stative verbs best describes this verb. If the verb is a dynamic verb, replace the base form with the present progressive. The first two sentences are done as examples.

The branch <u>break</u> under the weight of the snow.

ANSWER: Dynamic: The branch <u>is breaking</u> under the weight of the snow.

I <u>remember</u> what you told me.

ANSWER: Stative: I <u>remember</u> what you told me.

Category 1: Cognition and emotion

1. Nature <u>abhor</u> a vacuum. (saying)

_____

2. I <u>suppose</u> that the concert is at 8:00.

_____

3. John fill the car with gas while we get ready to go.

   _____

4. Everyone recognize the need to keep our costs down.

   _____

5. They visit her parents in Detroit this weekend.

   _____

6. He deserve better treatment than that!

   _____

7. She belong to a book club that meets once a month.

   _____

8. We sell what we can't take with us when we move.

   _____

9. This key fit the door to the garage.

   _____

10. Senator Blather announce his support for the trade agreement today.

   _____

Category 5, linking verbs with the meaning of appearance and sense perception, is different from the other four categories in that this category is not defined solely by meaning. It is also defined by its grammatical properties.

Linking verbs are a small (but very frequently used) group of verbs that have the unique characteristic of taking **predicate adjectives** and **predicate nominatives** as their **complements** (as opposed to **action verbs** that take **objects**). The complements always refer back to the subject, hence the term *linking* because the verb always connects or "links" the complement back to the subject. Here are some examples using the linking verb *be*:

> **Predicate adjective complements**
> Their son is quite tall for his age. (The predicate adjective *tall* refers back to the subject *their son*.)
> The performance was very enjoyable. (The predicate adjective *enjoyable* refers back to the subject *the performance*.)
>
> **Predicate nominative complements**
> Their son is a high school student. (The predicate noun *a high school student* refers back to the subject *their son*.)

The performance was a huge success. (The predicate noun *a huge success* refers back to the subject *the performance*.)

We can divide linking verbs into two classes: stative linking verbs and dynamic linking verbs. Here are some examples:

STATIVE LINKING VERBS	DYNAMIC LINKING VERBS
appear	become
be	get
feel	grow
look	prove
seem	remain
sound	stay
taste	turn

As you can see, stative linking verbs are the verb *be* (the most commonly used verb in English) and verbs of appearance and sense perception.

Here are some examples of both classes used in the present and present progressive tenses.

The verb *be* is almost always used as a stative verb. Here is what happens when we try to use *be* in the progressive tense:

    X Their son is being quite tall for his age.
    X The performance was being very enjoyable.
    X Their son is being a high school student.
    X The performance was being a huge success.

We can use *be* as a dynamic verb in the special sense of "deliberately perform or act as"; for example:

    Steven is being a total jerk.

The example sentence describes the way that Steven is acting at the moment. It does not mean that Steven is always a jerk. If we meant to say that, we would use the present tense:

    Steven is a total jerk.

Here are examples of some stative and dynamic linking verbs:

Stative linking verbs
Examples: appear, taste

Present tense	The situation appears to be getting worse.
Present progressive tense	**X** The situation is appearing to be getting worse.
Present tense	The coffee tastes good.
Present progressive tense	**X** The coffee is tasting good.

Dynamic linking verbs
Examples: become, get

Present tense	**X** Sally <u>becomes</u> a good tennis player.
Present progressive tense	Sally <u>is becoming</u> a good tennis player.
Present tense	**X** The situation <u>gets</u> worse as time passes.
Present progressive tense	The situation <u>is getting</u> worse as time passes.

1·4

All of the underlined verbs in the following sentences are linking verbs in their base forms. Decide whether the verbs are stative verbs or dynamic verbs, and then rewrite the verb in either its present tense or present progressive tense form as appropriate. The first two sentences are done as examples.

The job <u>prove</u> harder than I thought.

ANSWER: Dynamic: The job <u>is proving</u> harder than I thought.

He <u>appear</u> angry about something.

ANSWER: Stative: He <u>appears</u> angry about something.

1. The saw <u>get</u> too hot to operate.

   _____

2. His idea <u>sound</u> pretty good to me.

   _____

3. The weather <u>turn</u> bitterly cold with the wind and cloud cover.

   _____

4. The pizza <u>look</u> done.

   _____

5. I <u>be</u> ready to go whenever you are.

   _____

6. I <u>become</u> more and more optimistic about Aunt Mary's recovery.

   _____

7. The cloth <u>feel</u> too smooth to be wool.

   _____

8. His cooking <u>taste</u> terrible.

_____

9. The company <u>become</u> a highly successful operation.

_____

10. Uh-oh, the vegetables <u>smell</u> burned.

_____

The present tense

The present tense has a diverse range of meanings. There are no fewer than seven distinct meanings for the present tense distributed across not only present time but also past and future time as well. Here is a brief summary of the seven different meanings divided into three groups—the first group dealing with present time, the second group dealing with past time, and the third group dealing with future time:

Present time

1. Makes assertions or generalizations about ongoing conditions or states

2. Describes existing habits or customs

3. Comments on present-time actions

Past time

4. Recounts ideas or information from the past that affects us in the present

5. Comments on or paraphrases the works of others

Future time

6. Refers to future events if those events are fixed or scheduled

7. Refers to future events in adverb clauses when the main clause uses *will*

We will now discuss the present, past, and future uses of the present tense in detail.

Using the present tense for present time

Not surprisingly, the most common use of the present tense is for the present period of time. It is critical to understand that there are two fundamentally different ways of conceptualizing what we mean by "present time": (1) the present moment of time or (2) a span or period of time that is not bound to the present moment of time; that is, the verb describes an ongoing "timeless" state or condition.

If we want to refer to the present moment of time, we do not use the present tense at all; instead, we use the present progressive. If we want to refer to a span or period of present time, we use the present tense.

Here is an example that shows the difference between the two tenses:

Present progressive	Bill is walking the dog.
Present	Bill walks to help control his blood pressure.

The implication of the present progressive sentence is that Bill is out walking at this present moment of time. The present tense sentence does not tell us what Bill is doing at the moment. It tells us that Bill takes walks for his health, but it implies nothing about what Bill is doing at the present moment. In fact, Bill might not have walked for weeks.

EXERCISE
2·1

Each pair of sentences uses the same verb in its infinitive form (in parentheses). One of the sentences uses the verb to talk about an existing present condition; the other sentence uses the verb to talk about the present moment of time. Replace the verb in parentheses with the present tense if the verb is talking about an existing condition. Replace the verb in parentheses with the present perfect if the verb is talking about the present moment of time. The first is done as an example.

treat
Doctors (treat) this type of infection with broad-spectrum antibiotics.

is treating
The doctor (treat) the infection with a broad-spectrum antibiotic.

1. I can't see you. The light (shine) in my eyes.

   The light (shine) against the paintings on the wall.

2. The kids (play) in the living room.

   The kids (play) indoors when it rains.

3. The company (publish) my first novel.

   The company (publish) works by new authors.

4. Bad news always (spread) faster than good news.

   The news (spread) all over town.

5. We (gain) weight as we get older.

   We (gain) weight on this trip.

6. The board (make) the final decision on hiring.

   The board (make) a bad mistake.

7. Conflicts about immigration always (divide) communities.

   The conflict on immigration (divide) the community into factions.

8. The garage always (check) the oil.

   The mechanic (check) the oil now.

9. John (smile) whenever he thinks about what you said.

   John (smile) at what you just said.

10. We (walk) every chance we get.

    We (walk) to the park. Want to come along?

The present tense verbs that treat the present as a "timeless" span or period of time fall into two distinct categories: (1) verbs that make assertions or generalizations about ongoing conditions or states and (2) verbs that describe habits or customs. We will discuss both ways of treating present time.

Assertions or generalizations about ongoing conditions or states. As noted in Chapter 1, verbs in English (and most other languages, for that matter) can be divided into two large families: **dynamic** and **stative**; 99 percent of all verbs belong to the dynamic family. The traditional definition of verb (a word that shows action) refers exclusively to dynamic verbs. Dynamic verbs do things; for example: *run, jump, sing, work, sleep*.

Stative verbs, on the other hand, don't really do anything. Instead, they describe conditions or states. While there are only a relative handful of stative verbs, they are among the most frequently used verbs. For example, *be* and *have* are stative verbs. Here are some examples:

> *Be* Mary is cold.
>   Mary is a farmer.
> *Have* Mary has a little lamb.
>   The lamb has a ribbon around its neck.

In these example sentences, the subjects (*Mary* and the *lamb*) are not doing anything. Rather, the stative verbs *be* and *have* are used to describe or tell us something about the subjects.

The reason why the distinction between dynamic and stative verbs is relevant to this discussion is that the present tenses of *all* stative verbs make assertions or generalizations about presently existing conditions or states, and as such, they must be used in the present tense because that is what the function of the present tense is: to make assertions about ongoing conditions or states. In fact, if we try to use stative verbs in the present progressive, the result is predictably ungrammatical:

Be **X** Mary <u>is being</u> cold.
X Mary <u>is being</u> a farmer.
Have **X** Mary <u>is having</u> a little lamb.
X The lamb <u>is having</u> a ribbon around its neck.

The inherently different meanings of these two types of verbs cause them to interact very differently with the present tense. The timeless meaning of stative verbs is a perfect match with the timeless meaning of the present tense. Conversely, the time-bound meaning of dynamic verbs makes them incompatible with the basic "timeless" meaning of the present tense; for example, when we use the dynamic verb *buy* in the present, the result is ungrammatical:

X John <u>buys</u> a truck.

As we will see, we can make this and other dynamic verbs grammatical in the present tense, but only if we use them in sentences that make "timeless" assertions or generalizations, or use the verbs to describe habitual or customary actions.

Most stative verbs can be grouped into the following six semantic categories (with examples):

Appearance: appear, be, look, seem
Cognition: believe, know, mean, think, understand
Emotions: appreciate, desire, dislike, doubt, hate, like, need, prefer, want, wish
Measurement: consist of, contain, cost, have, measure, weight
Sense: feel, hear, see, seem, smell, taste
Ownership: belong, have, own, possess

(**Note:** some verbs appear twice because they can be used with different meanings.)

EXERCISE
2·2

The underlined verbs in the following sentences are all in the present tense. The sentences that use stative verbs are grammatical; the sentences that use dynamic verbs are ungrammatical. In the space provided, write "OK" if the sentence is grammatical; write "Not OK" if the sentence is not grammatical. The first two sentences are done as examples.

I <u>like</u> how you have arranged your office.

ANSWER: **OK**

        We <u>compare</u> the results from the two samples.

ANSWER: **Not OK**

1. I <u>shake</u> the tree to make the nuts fall off. _____

2. I <u>doubt</u> that we can get to the meeting on time. _____

3. The police <u>identify</u> the suspect. _____

4. His proposal <u>sounds</u> pretty attractive to me. _____

5. We <u>arrange</u> a meeting between the two groups. _____

6. I <u>gain</u> two pounds over the holiday. _____

7. We <u>know</u> what you mean. _____

8. The whole project <u>costs</u> more than we can afford to pay. _____

9. I <u>fill</u> the tank with gas. _____

10. The results in the study closely <u>resemble</u> the result predicted in the model.

    _____

11. When the water in the tank <u>equals</u> the water outside the tank, the gate will open.

    _____

12. Their lawyer <u>explains</u> the problem. _____

13. The job <u>entails</u> a great deal of travel. _____

14. I <u>watch</u> TV. _____

15. I <u>hear</u> what you are saying. _____

Dynamic verbs can also be used in the present tense, but only if one of the following two conditions on the meaning of the sentence are met: (1) the sentence makes an assertion or generalization about existing conditions or states, or (2) the sentence describes existing habits or customs. Let us take these conditions in order:

The assertions/generalizations can be of an objective, scientific nature; for example:

> The planets <u>revolve</u> around the sun.
> Fresh water <u>floats</u> on top of sea water.

They can be publicly verifiable; for example:

> The semesters at our school <u>last</u> 15 weeks.
> He <u>gives</u> private piano lessons.

They can be totally subjective personal opinions; for example:

> Kids today <u>spend</u> too much time playing computer games.
> Greenhouse gases <u>cause</u> global warming.
> Cable TV <u>costs</u> too much.

Notice that none of these examples of dynamic verbs is tied to a specific moment in time. All are essentially "timeless" generalizations.

Existing habits or customs. Here are some examples of verbs in this category:

> I always <u>take</u> my lunch to work.
> We <u>go</u> to the movies every chance we get.
> She normally <u>checks</u> her messages first thing in the morning.
> The westbound train <u>stops</u> here only in the morning.
> The kids usually <u>do</u> their homework right after school.

Verbs in this category describe a behavior that is typical or normal. It does not mean that the action is being performed at the present moment. For example:

> We usually <u>eat</u> dinner at my mother's house on Sunday.

This sentence does not mean that we are eating at my mother's house now. In fact, the sentence would still be a valid statement if we haven't seen my mother in a month.

One of the characteristics of this use of the present tense is that the sentence typically contains an adverb of frequency such as *usually, always, every day, normally*, or *every weekend*.

EXERCISE
2·3

All of the following sentences use the present tense of dynamic verbs, some sentences correctly, some incorrectly. If the sentence is grammatical, write "OK" in the space provided and then give the reason that justifies using the present tense. Use either "assertion" or "habitual." If the use of the present tense is ungrammatical, write "Not OK." The first three sentences are done as examples.

We usually <u>start</u> around 8:00.

ANSWER: OK habitual

I <u>ask</u> the same question.

ANSWER: Not OK

Cold winters <u>kill</u> the beetles that attack pine trees.

ANSWER: OK assertion

1. Eating too much always <u>makes</u> me sleepy.

---

2. Garlic <u>lowers</u> one's blood pressure.

   _____

3. The two parties <u>discuss</u> the agreement.

   _____

4. Research <u>proves</u> that listening to loud music permanently damages teenagers' hearing.

   _____

5. The janitor normally <u>locks</u> up after everyone leaves.

   _____

6. The flood waters <u>spread</u> throughout the valley.

   _____

7. The nurse <u>treats</u> the wound now.

   _____

8. Journalists never <u>tell</u> who their sources are.

   _____

9. The company <u>publishes</u> my first book.

   _____

10. Ravens and crows <u>recognize</u> people they have seen before.

    _____

Finally, there is a third use of the present tense that refers to present time. However, this use is completely different from the first two because this third use actually does refer to the present moment of time (unlike the other two already discussed). We can use the present tense to comment on or describe an ongoing present time action. Obviously, the situations in which we would use the present tense in this manner are highly restricted. The most common situations are sports events, demonstrations, and speech act commentaries. Here are some examples of each type:

Sports event	Here <u>comes</u> the pitch. Johnston <u>swings</u> and <u>misses</u>. Rodriguez <u>is</u> tripped in midfield. The referee <u>blows</u> his whistle and <u>gives</u> a yellow card to the defender.
Demonstration	Next, I <u>add</u> a cup of flour and <u>stir</u> in thoroughly. Finally, I <u>close</u> all open windows and <u>reboot</u> the computer.

Speech act commentary   I hereby <u>resign</u> from the council.
We <u>accept</u> your offer.

We have now identified three different ways present tense verbs refer to present time:
- ◆ By making assertions or generalizations about ongoing conditions or states
- ◆ By describing presently existing habits or customs
- ◆ By commenting on present-time ongoing actions

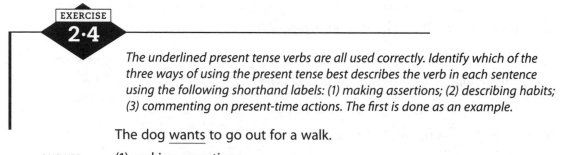

EXERCISE
2·4

The underlined present tense verbs are all used correctly. Identify which of the three ways of using the present tense best describes the verb in each sentence using the following shorthand labels: (1) making assertions; (2) describing habits; (3) commenting on present-time actions. The first is done as an example.

The dog <u>wants</u> to go out for a walk.

ANSWER: (1) making assertions

1. Clothes <u>dry</u> a lot faster in hot weather.

_____

2. Today I <u>announce</u> my candidacy for the presidency of the United States.

_____

3. Houston, we <u>have</u> a problem.

_____

4. This children's cereal <u>contains</u> nothing but sugar and refined carbohydrates.

_____

5. Smith <u>scores</u> from 10 feet out.

_____

6. Janet <u>gets</u> the weather forecast every morning before she decides what to wear.

_____

7. My wife always <u>reads</u> the ending of books first.

_____

8. I really <u>like</u> the food here.

_____

9. New cars <u>cost</u> a fortune to repair because of all the electronics they have in them.

_____

10. The company sends <u>cards</u> to all its employees at Christmas every year.

_____

11. First, we <u>combine</u> all the dry ingredients together in a large bowl.

_____

12. Many people <u>vote</u> for whoever promises to lower their taxes the most.

_____

13. Every night my father <u>locks</u> up the house before he goes to bed.

_____

14. The bus <u>is</u> late this morning.

_____

15. The pond <u>attracts</u> a lot of mosquitoes.

Using the present tense for past time

We use the present tense for referring to the past in two ways: (1) recounting ideas or information from the past that affects us in the present, and (2) commenting on or paraphrasing the works of others.

Recounting ideas or information from the past that affects us in the present

Normally, when we talk or write about specific events, we do so in the past tense. For example, virtually all novels and short stories are written in the past tense. As we will see in the next section of this chapter, the basic meaning of the past tense is that the action described in the past tense is finished—over and done with.

But what if we want to talk about something that happened in the past that directly affects us in the present moment of time? Suppose, for example, that you heard on the evening news that a bad storm was predicted for your area. You could tell other people about the threatening weather in either the past tense or the present tense:

Past tense	The evening news <u>said</u> that a big storm <u>was</u> coming.
Present tense	The evening news <u>says</u> that a big storm <u>is</u> coming.

There is no real difference in meaning, but there is a difference in emphasis: the present tense version is much more immediate and urgent.

Even where there is no sense of urgency, the present tense still implies that the information is new and immediate. For example, compare the following sentences:

Past tense	I <u>heard</u> that you might be moving.
Present tense	I <u>hear</u> that you might be moving.

The use of the present tense suggests that the information is new and relevant to the speaker.

We often use the present tense in discussing older material to emphasize that the content is still relevant to us in the present time. Here are some examples:

St. Paul <u>says</u>, "If I <u>have</u> not charity I am nothing."
Darwin <u>emphasizes</u> that the world <u>is</u> not a static place.
Shakespeare <u>says</u> that all the world <u>is</u> a stage.

Commenting on or paraphrasing the works of others

When we write about the works of others, we often write in the present tense. Reviews of books, plays, movies, and TV programs are typically written in the present tense. For example, here is a brief summary of *The Milagro Beanfield War*. Notice that all of the verbs are in the present tense.

This 1988 fable about community solidarity <u>takes</u> place in the small town of Milagro, New Mexico (population 426). The movie <u>revolves</u> around the attempt by a large corporation to buy enough land in this small town to develop a tourist resort. The main obstacle <u>is</u> Joe Mondragon. Joe <u>takes</u> water that <u>runs</u> by his land to irrigate a field of beans that he <u>plants</u>. Technically, the water <u>is</u> reserved for the corporation, setting in motion a conflict over water rights between the local residents and the corporation. Colorful local characters and beautiful New Mexico scenery along with an intelligent, good-natured script <u>make</u> this a highly successful film.

Reports and summaries are usually written in the present tense. For example, here is a summary of a company's leave policy:

Our current leave policy <u>makes</u> no distinction between vacation leave, sick leave, or personal time. All employees <u>have</u> a base of two weeks leave in their first year with the company. For each subsequent year of continuous employment, employees <u>gain</u> an additional day of leave. The maximum amount of leave that can be accumulated <u>is</u> three weeks per year.

Using the present tense for future time

There are two different grammatical constructions in which the present tense is used to refer to future time: one in main clauses and one in dependent adverb clauses.

In main clauses, we use the present tense to refer to future events if those events are already fixed or scheduled; for example:

> The full moon <u>occurs</u> Wednesday night.
> The train <u>departs</u> at 11:35.
> Tomorrow's *New York Times* <u>covers</u> the Senate race in California.
> Next Tuesday <u>is</u> the twenty-third.
> I <u>see</u> the dentist tomorrow at 11:00.

There is a colloquial extension of the use of the present tense for proposing a course of action; for example: "OK, here's the plan. I <u>pick</u> up Mary at work, you <u>get</u> the car, and we all <u>meet</u> at the restaurant." In effect, this is a tentative proposal for a schedule of future activities.

We use the present tense for asking questions about predictable future events; for example:

> When <u>does</u> the movie start?
> When <u>is</u> the tide full?
> What day of the week <u>is</u> Christmas this year?
> When <u>does</u> the kids' summer program begin?

We would not use the present tense for future events that are less than certain; for example:

> **X** It <u>rains</u> tomorrow.
> **X** I believe that Italy <u>wins</u> the World Cup.
> **X** Our CEO thinks that we <u>get</u> the contract.

EXERCISE

2·5

In all of the following sentences, the present tense is used to refer to the future. If the usage is appropriate, write "OK." If the usage is not appropriate, write "Not OK." The first two sentences are done as examples.

Your presentation <u>begins</u> at 3:30.

ANSWER: OK

The senator easily <u>wins</u> reelection.

ANSWER: Not OK

1. The exam <u>ends</u> in exactly 45 minutes.

   _____

2. He <u>washes</u> the dishes.

   _____

3. The gates <u>close</u> at 10:00 tonight.

   _____

4. Susan <u>finds</u> the missing car keys.

   _____

5. We <u>get</u> off the freeway if the traffic gets any worse.

   _____

6. The moon <u>rises</u> just after sunset.

   _____

7. In order to be competitive, the store <u>drops</u> its prices.

   _____

8. When <u>is</u> the game?

   _____

9. Mrs. Brown <u>returns</u> on Monday.

   _____

10. They <u>meet</u> in Los Angeles next week, I believe.

   _____

The other use of the present tense for future time is in adverb clauses when the main clause uses *will* to talk about future time; for example:

A neighbor will look after our cat, while we <u>are</u> away.
main clause   adverb clause

I will call you if I <u>hear</u> anything.
main clause   adverb clause

They will start work as soon as they <u>get</u> the necessary permits.
main clause   adverb clause

> They won't win the war even if they <u>win</u> this battle.
>   main clause   adverb clause

In all these examples it is very easy to see that the verb in the present tense form is referring to the future just as much as the verb in the main clause that uses *will*.

One of the characteristics of adverb clauses is that they are easily moved in front of the main clause. As a result, the present tense used for future time can come before the main clause with *will*; for example:

> While we <u>are</u> away, a neighbor will look after our cat.
>   adverb clause   main clause

> If I <u>hear</u> anything, I will call you.
>   adverb clause   main clause

> As soon as they <u>get</u> the necessary permits, they will start work.
>   adverb clause   main clause

> Even if they <u>win</u> this battle, they won't win the war.
>   adverb clause   main clause

Note that when an adverb clause is moved from its normal position following the main clause and placed in front of the main clause, the adverb clause is set off from the main clause by a comma. This use of the comma is obligatory.

EXERCISE

2·6

The following sentences contain both a main clause and an adverb clause (in either order), with blank spaces where the verbs go. Underneath each sentence are two verbs in their infinitive forms. Insert the verbs into the appropriate clauses as directed. Make sure that each verb is used in the correct form to refer to future time. The first sentence is done as an example. Hint: the adverb clause always begins with an adverb or adverb phrase (for example: when, if, before).

Whatever they <u>need</u> us to do, we <u>will do</u>.

main clause: <u>do</u>; adverb clause: <u>need</u>

1. If I _____ him, I _____ hello.

   main clause: <u>say</u>; adverb clause: <u>see</u>

2. Until they _____ some more money, they _____ trouble paying for it.

   main clause: <u>have</u>; adverb clause: <u>save</u>

3. We definitely _____ if they _____ us the job.

   main clause: <u>accept</u>; adverb clause: <u>offer</u>

4. As soon I _____ home, I _____ dinner.

   main clause: <u>start</u>; adverb clause: <u>get</u>

5. We _____ a movie after we _____ eating.

   main clause: <u>watch</u>; adverb clause: <u>finish</u>

6. Once I _____ my check, I _____ for a new apartment.

   main clause: <u>look</u>; adverb clause: <u>get</u>

7. The game still _____ played, even if it _____.

   main clause: <u>be</u>; adverb clause: <u>rain</u>

8. We _____ ahead as planned, even though there _____ some objections.

   main clause: <u>go</u>; adverb clause: <u>be</u>

9. Unless there _____ a problem, we _____ you in Denver tomorrow.

   main clause: <u>meet</u>; adverb clause: <u>be</u>

10. I _____ to visit them next time I _____ to Phoenix.

    main clause: <u>try</u>; adverb clause: <u>go</u>

In this section we have identified the following seven meanings and uses of the present tense (numbered for use in the following exercise):

Present time

1. Makes assertions or generalizations about ongoing conditions or states

2. Describes existing habits or customs

3. Comments on present-time actions

Past time

4. Recounts ideas or information from the past that affects us in the present

5. Comments on or paraphrases the works of others

Future time

6. Refers to future events if those events are fixed or scheduled

7. Refers to future events in adverb clauses when the main clause uses *will*

EXERCISE
2·7

Each one of the following sentences contains an underlined present tense verb. Identify which of the seven uses best describes the meaning and use of that present tense verb using the numbers previously given. The first is done as an example.

The weather <u>seems</u> unusually hot for this time of year. (1)

1. Hurry up! The game <u>starts</u> in five minutes. _____

2. Anne's white paper <u>warns</u> against the risk of inflation. _____

3. As Freud <u>says</u>, "Sometimes a cigar is only a cigar." _____

4. In his essay, Whitehill <u>argues</u> for a return to the gold standard. _____

5. Good advance planning <u>saves</u> a lot of time in the long run. _____

6. Hardship <u>teaches</u> self-reliance. _____

7. I usually <u>decline</u> getting the extended warranties on things I buy. _____

8. When we <u>know</u> the date, we will send out the invitations. _____

9. I hereby <u>nominate</u> Joe Smith for Congress. _____

10. Raising children <u>requires</u> a lot of patience. _____

11. We <u>fly</u> back to Madison on Wednesday. _____   _____

12. My mother always <u>saves</u> empty plastic containers. _____

13. The goalie <u>blocks</u> a hard shot from the left corner. _____

14. The pilots will take off just as soon as they <u>get</u> clearance. _____

15. Darwin's research <u>rests</u> on a wealth of observational studies. _____

The past tense

The main use of the past tense is for events, conditions, or states that once existed in or during some past time but that do not exist in the present. There are two other non-past-time uses for the past tense: (1) hypothetical statements and (2) polite questions and deferential requests.

Using the past tense for past time

The past tense is used for events, conditions, or states that are now over and done with. So, for example:

> Samantha <u>went</u> to school at Berkeley.

This sentence not only tells us where Samantha went to school but also tells us that Samantha is no longer going to school there.

The past tense is quite broad in the sense that it can refer to variety of past-time uses; for example:

A single point of past time
The power <u>went</u> out at 7:15 this morning.
I <u>picked</u> up the kids after school.

A span of time
I <u>worked</u> in that office from 2001 to 2006.
The most recent ice age <u>lasted</u> for about 13,000 years.

Habitual or repeated events
We always <u>got</u> the *New York Times* when we lived in the city.
They <u>went</u> to the same hotel every anniversary.

States or conditions that existed at some past time
Jason always <u>admired</u> his father's achievements.
I <u>hated</u> having to take piano lessons when I was in grade school.

In all these different uses of the past tense, there is always the implication that it is no longer true today. Even ongoing states and conditions are tied (and limited) to the past. For example:

The children <u>loved</u> being read to at bedtime.

This sentence implies that the children are no longer being read to: either they have outgrown being read to or for some other reason no one reads to them anymore.

Other uses of the past tense

There are two other uses of the past tense:

- ◆ Hypothetical statements
- ◆ Polite questions and deferential requests

We will discuss these two uses of the past tense in turn.

Hypothetical statements

The past tense in modern English has inherited some of the functions of the subjective mood that existed in older forms of the language. One of these functions is making statements that are hypothetical or even contrary to fact. Needless to say, the past tense form in this subjunctive use does not mean past time; quite the contrary: this use of the subjunctive is often used to talk about the present or future (but in a tentative, hypothetical way).

The most distinctive use of the past tense for hypothetical statements is seen in constructions that preserve the historical subjunctive use of *were* instead of the expected *was*. Here are some examples:

> If I <u>were</u> you, I would try harder.
> I wish I <u>were</u> feeling better.
> It's not as though he <u>were</u> guilty of a crime.
> Suppose we <u>were</u> to quit our jobs.

If clauses have an unusual feature: all the verbs in the main clause that accompany the adverbial *if* clause must also be in the past tense. Here is an example of an *if* clause with multiple verbs in the main clause:

> If I <u>were</u> you, I <u>would</u> be careful of what I <u>said</u>.
>   main clause

Both verbs in the main clause, *would* and *said*, are in the past tense. In fact, if the verbs in the main clause were in the present or future tense, the sentence would become ungrammatical:

| *Present tense* | **X** If I <u>were</u> you, I <u>am</u> careful of what I <u>say</u>. |
| *Future tense* | **X** If I <u>were</u> you, I <u>will be</u> careful of what I <u>will say</u>. |

This is the only instance in English in which the subordinate clause controls the verb tense of the main clause.

Add the hypothetical if *clause* if I were you *to the following sentences, making the necessary changes to the verb tenses in the main clause. The first sentence is done as an example.*

I will tell them what they need to do.

ANSWER: If I were you, I <u>would</u> tell them what they <u>needed</u> to do.

1. I will watch what I eat.

_____

2. I will talk only about what I know.

_____

3. I will remind them what they agree to pay.

_____

4. I will be worried about where I park my car.

_____

5. I will start working only when I have enough light to see what I am doing.

_____

Polite questions and deferential requests

The past tense also inherits another feature of the subjunctive: deference or polite indirectness. This form of the subjunctive is used in asking questions and making requests when we want to show consideration or even polite deference to the person we are talking to. The use of the past tense form signals the person we are talking to that that person has no obligation to agree to or approve our request (which is put in the form of a question). Another way to think of it is that we are signaling that we are not acting as a superior talking to a subordinate as might be the implication of a direct question in the present tense. For example, if we were talking to friends or social equals, we would probably invite them to lunch in the present tense:

<u>Do</u> you want to go out for lunch?

However, if we were talking to a superior or a person we did not know well, we would probably phrase the invitation in a more indirect manner using the past tense:

Did you want to go out for lunch today?

Here is another example. We would probably ask a colleague for some time by saying:

Can you give me a minute?

But we would make the same request of a superior in the past tense:

Could you give me a minute?

We would ask equals if they were ready to leave in the present tense:

Are you ready to leave?

But we would ask a superior the same thing in the past tense:

Were you ready to leave?

EXERCISE

3·2

Here are ordinary questions that one might ask of equals. Change the questions to the corresponding polite or deferential form. The first sentence is done as an example:

Do you need to get something?

ANSWER: Did you need to get something?

1. What do you think about it?

_____

2. Will you join us for lunch?

_____

3. Can you stop by my office before you leave?

_____

4. Will you be free this evening?

_____

5. May I make an alternative proposal?

_____

The future tense

In traditional grammar, the future tense consists of the helping verb *will* followed by a verb in its **base form**. The base form of a verb is the dictionary entry form of the verb. It is an infinitive without the *to*; for example:

> I <u>will call</u> you as soon as I get a chance.

In this example, *call* is in its base form. *Will* plus the base-form verb *call* is thus the future tense of *call*.

The way traditional grammar defines the future tense (helping verb plus a base-form verb) is radically different from the way that the present and past tenses are defined. The present and past tenses are defined by a change in the verb itself, either by adding an ending (-*s* in the case of the present; -*ed* in the case of the past tense) or by a change in the form of the verb, as in the case of irregular verbs. To understand the implications of the traditional definition of the future tense, we need to understand a bit about the very peculiar history of the future tense in English.

At a distant time in the past, the ancestor language of English (called Indo-European) formed the future tense as all other verb tenses: by a change in the verb itself. This future tense is related to the future tenses that survive today in most modern-day languages of Indo-European origin, for example, French, Italian, Greek, Russian, and the languages of northern India.

Later, the common Indo-European language broke apart into separate branches. The branch that ultimately leads to English is Germanic (the Germanic languages besides English are Dutch, German, and the Scandinavian languages). One of the main characteristics of the Germanic branch that sets it apart from all the other branches of Indo-European is that the future tense verb ending totally disappeared. That is, none of the Germanic languages (including English) has a verb tense form that means future time.

The disappearance of the future tense verb form in the ancestral Germanic language was probably the result of another development unique to the Germanic languages: the creation of a remarkable set of helping verbs called **modal verbs.** These modal verbs provided speakers with a more

33

sophisticated and flexible way of talking about the future. It is entirely likely that the future verb tense form was driven into extinction by the rise of these modal verbs. The modern English forms of the modal verbs are the following: *can, may, must, shall,* and *will.*

These five verbs can all be used with infinitives to talk about the future:

> I can call him later.
> I may call him later.
> I must call him later.
> I shall call him later.
> I will call him later.

We can even use the past tense forms of these verbs (except *must*, which has no past tense) to talk about the future:

> I could call him later.
> I might call him later.
> I should call him later.
> I would call him later if I were you.

As you can see, these nine verb forms allow English speakers to talk about the future in a number of highly nuanced ways—much more than a single future tense verb form would ever allow.

If all of these helping verbs have evolved to become the way that English speakers talk about future time, then why was *will* singled out by traditional grammar as "the future tense" in English? There are two reasons: (1) *will* is the closest in meaning of all nine modal forms to the meaning of the future tense in Latin (Latin is the basis of traditional grammars of English), and (2) the basic meaning of *will* is simple futurity; all of the other modal verbs have a variety of additional meanings such as necessity, possibility, and obligation. Because Latin has nothing similar to modal verbs, traditional Latin-based grammars of English simply ignored the remaining modal verbs.

In this chapter we will examine *will* because (1) it is the traditional marker of the future tense, and (2) it is by far the most common way of talking about future time. We will also examine the four nonmodal ways that English speakers commonly use to refer to future time.

Using *will* to talk about future time

We use *will* in two quite different ways: (1) prediction and (2) intention.

Will is used to make predictions about some future event, behavior, or outcome. Here are some examples:

> The weatherman says that it will rain all day tomorrow.
> You will feel better after a good night's sleep.

The stock market will react negatively to such bad economic news.
They will never agree to such a proposal.
Who knows how soon the volcano will erupt again?
Will the store be open on Sunday?

We can also use *will* in a somewhat different way to talk about characteristic behaviors or actions (which, of course, we predict will reoccur in the future); for example:

Sally will play with that toy all day.
They will end up arguing about politics as usual.
My father will want to pick up the check.
The market will, as usual, overreact to any unexpected development.
On vacation we will get up late every morning and go for a walk before breakfast.

Will is also used to make a statement of someone's intention to carry out some future action. This use of *will* requires an animate subject that acts volitionally to carry out a purposeful future act. Here are some examples:

I will give you a hand with that.
He will call you back as soon as he gets a chance.
I will stop by after work if it is not too late.
Jerry will never allow that to happen.
The company will petition the court for an injunction to stop the strike.

This meaning of *will* is used for requests for future actions and questions about a person's intentions or willingness to do something in the future; for example:

Will you answer the phone?
Will you set the table, please?
Will you be able to attend the meeting?
Will the union cooperate?

Will used as an expression of intention is often replaced in questions or requests by *would* as a form of respect or politeness; for example:

Will/would you help me with this?
Will/would that be OK with you?
Will/would you take care of that?
Would you like to dance?

(For a detailed discussion of polite questions and deferential requests, see Chapter 3, "The past tense.")

All of the sentences that follow contain will *(or the polite form* would*) used for talking about future time. Identify whether* will/would *is used for prediction or intention. The first two sentences are done as examples.*

The traffic <u>will</u> be really bad when we go to the airport.

ANSWER: Prediction

I <u>will</u> <u>get</u> us some more coffee.

ANSWER: Intention

1. I think that the committee <u>will</u> not approve his application the way it is written now.

    _____

2. The maintenance staff <u>will have</u> finished by now.

    _____

3. We <u>will</u> certainly <u>do</u> our best to meet your expectations.

    _____

4. <u>Would</u> you <u>like</u> to leave a message?

    _____

5. They are so good that I think they <u>will qualify</u> for the World Cup this year.

    _____

6. I <u>will go</u> home the back way so you can see the river.

    _____

7. The lawyer thinks that they <u>will settle</u> out of court.

    _____

8. We <u>would like</u> some more coffee, please.

    _____

9. You <u>will have</u> a hard time selling the house in this economy.

_____

10. I <u>will think</u> about it.

_____

Other ways of talking about future time

There are four nonmodal ways to talk about future time:

- ◆ Present progressive tense
- ◆ Present tense
- ◆ *Be going to* plus base form
- ◆ *Be about to* plus base form

The present progressive and present tenses are similar in meaning, but the present progressive tense is much broader in its use than the present tense. We will discuss the present progressive tense first, then we will turn to the more restricted present tense, and finally we will discuss the differences and similarities between these two ways of talking about the future.

Present progressive tense

The present progressive tense refers to future events that arise directly (and often immediately) from present plans, arrangements, or commitments; for example:

> We <u>are continuing</u> the presentation after lunch.
> The children <u>are going</u> to the park this afternoon.
> They <u>are taking</u> a taxi to the airport.
> The president <u>is making</u> a speech here next month.
> My parents <u>are staying</u> in Arizona this winter.

As you can see from these examples, the present progressive tense is often used with animate subjects; these subjects are the ones who make the plans, the arrangements, or the commitments that cause the future action. The present progressive can also be used with inanimate subjects, but only if the action or event is arranged, scheduled, or highly predictable; for example:

> The play <u>is opening</u> Friday night.
> According to the weather channel, it'<u>s getting</u> warmer tomorrow.
> The trains <u>are running</u> on a holiday schedule Monday.
> The cherry trees in Washington <u>are blooming</u> next week.
> Our team <u>is playing</u> at home next week.

There is one important restriction on the use of the present progressive: many stative verbs cannot be used in the present progressive. Here are some examples with stative verbs:

X We <u>are needing</u> to change trains at the next station.
X They <u>are wanting</u> to talk to us.
X The kids <u>are feeling</u> bad if we don't come.

We often use the present progressive for announcing imminent actions or events; for example:

We <u>are ordering</u> takeout; let me know what you want.
Your coffee <u>is getting</u> cold.
Kids, <u>we're leaving</u> soon.
Come to the table; <u>we're eating</u> in just a minute.
Hurry, the game <u>is starting</u> right after this commercial.
The market <u>is opening</u> in five minutes.

Present tense

The present tense can refer to future events, but only if those events have already been determined. It is the tense we would use for scheduled or fixed events; for example:

Jayne's wedding <u>is</u> June 18.
Our plane <u>departs</u> at 8:15.
I <u>see</u> the dentist next Tuesday.
They <u>get</u> back next week.
The plays there <u>start</u> at 8:30.

We cannot use the present tense for unscheduled future actions or events; for example:

X It <u>rains</u> tomorrow.
X They <u>are</u> upset if we don't get the contract.
X I <u>come</u> back early unless there is a problem.
X We <u>go</u> home soon.

The use of the present tense for future time is more restricted than the present progressive. For example, all of the following sentences in the present progressive are grammatical:

We <u>are ordering</u> takeout; let me know what you want.
Your coffee <u>is getting</u> cold.
Kids, we <u>are leaving</u> now.
Come to the table; we <u>are eating</u> in just a minute.
Hurry, the game <u>is starting</u> right after this commercial.
The market <u>is opening</u> in a few minutes.

When we use the present tense in these same examples, the results are surprisingly diverse: some (marked with **X**) are flatly ungrammatical, some (marked with **?**) are probably grammatical but sound odd, and some are perfectly grammatical:

> **X** We <u>order</u> takeout; let me know what you want.
> **X** Your coffee <u>gets</u> cold.
> **?** Kids, we <u>leave</u> now.
> **?** Come to the table; we <u>eat</u> in just a minute.
> Hurry, the game <u>starts</u> right after this commercial.
> The market <u>opens</u> in a few minutes.

The degree of grammaticality in using the present tense is a function of how formally the future event is scheduled. In the first two examples, there is no scheduling or planning at all; they are extemporaneous, unplanned statements about the future, and, as such, they are clearly incompatible with the present tense:

> **X** We <u>order</u> takeout; let me know what you want.
> **X** Your coffee <u>gets</u> cold.

The last two examples refer to formally scheduled future events:

> Hurry, the game <u>starts</u> right after this commercial.
> The market <u>opens</u> in a few minutes.

These are completely grammatical in the present tense.

The middle two examples are in between planned and unplanned. That is, they are not formally planned, but they are not really extemporaneous either. The borderline grammaticality of these two sentences reflects the fact that they are quasi-planned.

> **?** Kids, we <u>leave</u> now.
> **?** Come to the table; we <u>eat</u> in just a minute.

Here is another pair of sentences that illustrates the difference between the present and present progressive for future time:

Present	**X** I <u>take</u> a group picture after class.
Present progressive	I <u>am taking</u> a group picture after class.

Both of these sentences are talking about carrying out a future-time activity. The problem with using the present tense is that the activity is not formally scheduled. Its extemporaneous nature makes it incompatible with the present tense. Using the present tense this way is a common mistake for even advanced nonnative speakers of English.

The much tighter restrictions on the use of the present tense mean that many verbs that can be used quite normally in the present progressive for future time cannot be used in the present tense.

All of the following sentences contain grammatical uses of the present progressive tense. Change each use of the present progressive into the present tense, and then determine the grammatical validity of the result. If the result is fully grammatical, write "OK." If the result is not grammatical or is distinctly odd, write "Not OK." The first two sentences are done as examples.

She <u>is having</u> a baby next June.

ANSWER: She <u>has</u> a baby next June. Not OK

She <u>is going</u> into the hospital next week.

ANSWER: She <u>goes</u> into the hospital next week. OK

1. Everyone <u>is staying</u> with friends until the water recedes.

_____

2. They <u>are moving</u> out of the apartment at the end of the month.

_____

3. I <u>am waxing</u> the car as soon as the water dries.

_____

4. We <u>are helping</u> the public radio fund-raising program Saturday from noon till 4:00.

_____

5. Loretta <u>is presenting</u> the keynote at this year's conference.

_____

6. They <u>are selling</u> their house as soon as they get a reasonable offer.

_____

7. The course <u>is covering</u> that material in the last week.

_____

8. Because of global warming, some insurance companies <u>are raising</u> their flood insurance rates next year.

_____

9. The contractor <u>is laying</u> the carpet as soon as he can get the pad installed.

_____

10. I <u>am teaching</u> that class next semester.

_____

The difference we have seen between present progressive and present tense carries over to situations in which both the present progressive and present tenses are grammatical. For example, compare the following sentences:

Present progressive	Our flight <u>is leaving</u> at 8:15.
Present	Our flight <u>leaves</u> at 8:15.

These two sentences mean the same thing, but there is a difference in their implications. Using the present progressive implies that this is new information: either it is new information to the person being spoken to, or the original flight departure time has been changed, and thus it is new information for everybody. If it is the latter, there is the additional implication that this new time is not firmly scheduled and is thus subject to further change.

Using the present tense implies that the flight is definitely scheduled to leave at 8:15. If this is a new time, it implies that this new time is a formal rescheduling of the original departure time, and as such we have some expectation that this departure time is reliable information.

Finally, we need to mention another, unrelated use of the present tense for future time. We use it in adverb clauses when the main clause uses *will* to indicate future time; for example:

If she <u>pushes</u> this button, the outdoor lights <u>will</u> go on.
    adverb clause   main clause

When he <u>moves</u> there next month, he <u>will</u> need to get new furniture.
    adverb clause   main clause

The adverb and main clause can be used in either order:

The outdoor lights <u>will</u> go on if she <u>pushes</u> this button.
        main clause   adverb clause

He <u>will</u> need to get new furniture when he <u>moves</u> there next month.
main clause   adverb clause

See Chapter 2 for a detailed discussion of this rather specialized use of the present tense.

Be going to plus base form

This idiomatic construction uses some form of *be* in the present tense to express future action; for example:

> I am going to take the 5:45 train.
> The price of gold is going to fall dramatically.

An alternative analysis would be to describe this construction as follows:

> *be going* plus infinitive

An infinitive consists of *to* plus a base-form verb. Obviously, either description will work. The reason that linguists prefer *be going to* plus base-form verb is that is it easy to break the construction apart between the *to* and the base-form verb, suggesting that the *to* is more like a preposition than the marker of an infinitive. Here is a brief dialogue that separates the *to* from the base-form verb:

> A: Do you think George will ever retire?
> B: Yes, I think he actually is going to this summer. (*Retire* is understood.)

If *to retire* were a single grammatical unit, we would not expect to separate the *to* and *retire* so easily.

Here are some more examples of this construction:

> Aunt Mae and Uncle Jim are going to sell the farm.
> The storm is going to hit sometime tomorrow morning.
> Our mayor is going to run for Congress this fall.

When the subject is an animate noun, *be going to* plus base-form verb signals a strong intention of the subject to carry out the future action specified, almost as a statement of commitment. Here are some more examples with animate subjects:

> We are going to get married.
> The company is going to open a new branch in Seattle.
> They are going to meet us at the park.
> I am going to mow the lawn now.

With inanimate subjects, the speaker is asserting confidence that the described future event is highly likely to actually happen; for example:

> It's going to start raining any minute.
> The reception is going to be at her aunt's house.
> His speech is going to create a lot of controversy.
> The train is going to be half an hour late.

We can even use this construction with non-referential, existential subjects like *there* and *it* as long as the speaker has confidence in the validity of what is said:

There is going to be a staff meeting Friday.
It's going to be really hot tomorrow.

Be about to plus base form

This is another idiomatic construction that also uses some form of *be* in the present tense to express future action; for example:

Hurry, the light is about to change.
Let's sit down. The presentation is about to begin.
I'm about to give up.
The boat is about to leave.

The *to* in this construction also acts as a preposition rather than the marker of an infinitive because we can so easily separate the *to* and the verb; for example:

A: Are you going to quit soon?
B: Yes, I am just about to. (*Quit* is understood.)

Be about to plus base form is used to emphasize that something is on the verge of happening. It is used to emphasize the immediacy of what is going to happen in the very near future. *Be about to* plus base form can be used only with verbs that convey a strong sense of immediate action. As we would expect, this construction is most often used with verbs that have animate subjects that perform the action of the verb; for example:

John is about to look for a new job.
The company is about to open a new plant in Mexico.
Can't it wait? We're just about to leave.
The president is about to make an important announcement.
We are about to buy our first new car.

Be about to plus base form can be used with inanimate subjects, but only if there is a sense of immediacy in the sentence. The action does not need to be caused by the subject of the sentence. Here are some examples:

The house is about to go on the market.
Their job description is about to change drastically.
The field is about to be flooded for irrigation.

We can also use impersonal subjects; for example:

It's about to start raining.
There is about to be a big fight over the proposed new law.

Summary of ways of talking about the future

In this chapter we have identified the following six different ways of talking about the future:

- *Will* plus base form (prediction)

Animate	They <u>will call</u> us as soon as they hear anything.
Inanimate	It <u>will take</u> about 45 minutes to get to the airport.

- *Will* plus base form (intention)

Animate	I <u>will take</u> you to the airport.
Inanimate	(rarely used)

  Comment: *will* plus base form is used for normal expectations about future actions or events.

- Present progressive tense

Animate	I <u>am taking</u> them to the airport.
Inanimate	The meeting <u>is starting</u> at 4:30.

  Comment: with animate nouns, the present progressive refers to future events that arise directly from present plans, arrangements, or commitments. With inanimate nouns, the present progressive refers to events that are arranged or highly predictable. We often use the present progressive for announcing imminent actions or events, especially if the actions or events are new information.

- Present tense

Animate	Alice <u>takes</u> the kids to camp tomorrow.
Inanimate	Their flight <u>leaves</u> at 6:30.

  Comment: the present tense is used to describe an action or event that has been scheduled or prearranged.

- *Be going to* plus base form

Animate	I'm <u>going to give</u> them a call right now.
Inanimate	Their flight <u>is going to be</u> a little late.

  Comment: with animate nouns, *be going to* plus base form signals a strong intention or even commitment to carry out a future action. With inanimate nouns, *be going to* plus base form asserts confidence that the described future event will actually happen.

- *Be about to* plus base form

Animate	They <u>are about to board</u> their plane.
Inanimate	The plane <u>is about to take</u> off.

Comment: with both animate and inanimate subjects, *be about to* plus base form emphasizes the immediacy of the action of the verb.

In deciding what form to use for talking about future time, here are some things to keep in mind:

- *Will* plus base form is the default way of talking about the future. That is, we use *will* plus base form unless we have a particular reason for using one of the other forms.
- The present progressive and *be going to* plus base form are used very frequently in conversation because they both imply information that is new to the audience. For example, compare the following uses of *will* plus base form, present progressive, and *be going to* plus base form:

Will plus base form	I'll take the bus to work tomorrow.
Present progressive	I'm taking the bus to work tomorrow.
Be going to plus base form	I'm going to take the bus to work tomorrow.

All three sentences have the same basic meaning. However, they do not have the same implications. The use of *will* plus base form implies that taking the bus to work is something that the speaker does frequently so that the sentence is merely confirming a normal practice. Both the present progressive and the *be going to* plus base form, however, are announcing something that is new to the audience and/or is worth singling out for special emphasis.

Here is the opposite situation where the "new information" aspect of the present progressive and *be going to* plus base form are inappropriate. Imagine it's the end of the workday; two colleagues are leaving the office at the same time, and each says "good-bye" to the other with the following verb forms:

Will plus base form	I'll see you tomorrow.
Present progressive	I'm seeing you tomorrow.
Be going to plus base form	I'm going to see you tomorrow.

The "new information" verb forms are utterly socially inappropriate because they (incorrectly) imply that seeing the other person at work the next day is the result of some special arrangement; it is not something that just normally happens.

- The remaining two verb forms, present tense and *be about to* plus base form, are essentially special-purpose verb forms: the present tense is used solely for future events that are already scheduled or fixed; *be about to* plus base form is used to emphasize the immediacy of the future action or event.

To summarize:

- ◆ Normal expectations about future actions or events: *will* plus base form
- ◆ New information about future actions or events: present progressive or *be going to* plus base form
- ◆ Scheduled or fixed future events: present tense
- ◆ Immediate future actions or events: *be about to* plus base form

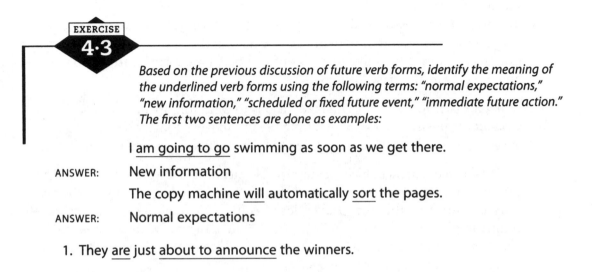

EXERCISE
4·3

Based on the previous discussion of future verb forms, identify the meaning of the underlined verb forms using the following terms: "normal expectations," "new information," "scheduled or fixed future event," "immediate future action." The first two sentences are done as examples:

I <u>am going to go</u> swimming as soon as we get there.

ANSWER: New information

The copy machine <u>will</u> automatically <u>sort</u> the pages.

ANSWER: Normal expectations

1. They <u>are</u> just <u>about to announce</u> the winners.

_____

2. The play <u>closes</u> after Saturday's performance.

_____

3. The days <u>will be</u> longer in April.

_____

4. We <u>are staying</u> a few nights in Paris on our way back.

_____

5. They <u>are about to make</u> a really big mistake.

_____

6. The new law <u>goes</u> into effect tomorrow.

_____

7. Remember, I <u>present</u> the committee's recommendations to the board on Friday.

_____

8. Naturally, they <u>will resist</u> any last-minute changes.

_____

9. I <u>am about to leave</u>; do you want a ride?

_____

10. They <u>are selling</u> their house as soon as they can get a buyer.

_____

EXERCISE

4·4

Based on the previous discussion of future verb forms, pick the best future-time form for the underlined verb to represent the future-time meanings that appear in parentheses. The first two sentences are done as examples.

(normal expectations) I <u>believe</u> that when I see it.

ANSWER: I <u>will believe</u> that when I see it.

(new information) We <u>make</u> them a new offer.

ANSWER: We <u>are making/are going to make</u> them a new offer.

1. (immediate future action) Careful, you <u>sit</u> in a wet chair.

_____

2. (scheduled or fixed future event) The tournament <u>begin</u> this Saturday.

_____

3. (new information) I <u>need</u> to rent a car.

_____

4. (normal expectations) I <u>turn</u> the lights off when I leave the building.

_____

5. (immediate future action) We <u>replace</u> the countertops in the kitchen.

_____

6. (new information) They <u>launch</u> a search for the overdue hikers.

   _____

7. (scheduled or fixed future event) The news <u>come</u> on at 10:00 tonight.

   _____

8. (immediate future action) The storm <u>hit</u> the coast with heavy rains.

   _____

9. (normal expectations) The aides <u>handle</u> all the registration details.

   _____

10. (new information) He <u>try</u> a totally new approach.

   _____

Introduction to the perfect tenses

What is so "perfect" about the perfect tenses? Nothing. The use of *perfect* as a grammatical term comes from the Latin verb *perficere*, "to do something completely or to bring something to a successful completion." The modern English word *perfect* is normally used as an adjective, but we still keep one of the original Latin verb meanings of *perficere*, "to bring to a successful completion." For example, a tennis player might say, "I am trying to perfect my backhand." (Note: The verb *perfect* is even pronounced differently from the adjective *perfect*. The verb is stressed on the second syllable, "perFECT," while the adjective is stressed on the first syllable, "PERfect.") Over time the English verb *perfect* developed a secondary meaning of "to finish or complete." It is this meaning that the grammatical term *perfect* draws on: the perfect tenses have a stated or implied finishing point.

There are three perfect tenses: the **present perfect**, the **past perfect**, and the **future perfect**. All three are formed in exactly parallel manner: the appropriate present, past, or future tense form of the helping verb *have* followed by a verb in the past participle form; for example:

Present perfect	Joan has lived in Denver for five years.
Past perfect	Joan had lived in Denver for five years before she moved last May.
Future perfect	Joan will have lived in Denver for five years this May.

The most common use of the **present perfect** is for past-time actions or events whose actions or consequences continue until they are terminated, i.e., "perfected," at the present moment of time.

Joan has lived in Denver for five years.

In our example sentence, the use of the present perfect *has lived* means that Joan moved to Denver five year ago and has continued to live in Denver right up to the present moment of time.

The **past perfect** is used for some more distant past time, or past actions or events that were terminated, "perfected," at some more recent moment of past time, or by some more recent past-time event.

> Joan <u>had lived</u> in Denver for five years before she moved last May.

In our example sentence, the use of the past perfect *had lived* means that Joan lived in Denver for five years until she moved in May. Joan's moving in May is the more recent past-time event that terminated the action of the past perfect verb *had lived*.

The **future perfect** is used for future-time actions or events that will be terminated, "perfected," by an even more distant moment of time or defining event.

> Joan <u>will have lived</u> in Denver for five years this May.

In our example sentence, the use of the present perfect *will have lived* means that as of this coming May, Joan has lived in Denver for five years. *This May* is the more distant future-time expression that terminates the action of the future perfect verb *will have lived*.

EXERCISE
5·1

Underline and identify the perfect tenses in the following sentences. The first is done as an example.

We had just finished dinner when the phone rang.

ANSWER: We <u>had</u> just <u>finished</u> dinner when the phone rang.
past perfect

1. Fortunately, I had checked the weather before we started on the hike.

   _____

2. The storm has delayed all inbound flights.

   _____

3. By then, the market will have closed.

   _____

4. During the night, the electricity had gone out so the clocks were all wrong.

   _____

5. It looks as though they have already started on the project.

_____

6. Fortunately, I had gotten some euros before I flew to Rome.

_____

7. Some politicians have maintained friendships with members of the opposing party.

_____

8. We hope that we will have finished by noon.

_____

9. No one had anticipated how difficult the problem would be.

_____

10. The resistance movement will have armed itself as soon as they heard the news.

_____

Replace the underlined infinitive verb with the perfect verb form identified in parentheses. The first is done as an example.

(past perfect) They <u>hire</u> extra security for the concert.

ANSWER: They <u>had hired</u> extra security for the concert.

1. (present perfect) I <u>ask</u> them to provide more information.

_____

2. (future perfect) Surely the lake <u>freeze</u> by now.

_____

3. (past perfect) We <u>tell</u> them about what they said.

_____

4. (future perfect) They <u>clear</u> customs by now.

_____

5. (present perfect) The court <u>rule</u> on many similar cases over the years.

_____

6. (past perfect) Before they moved in, they <u>repaint</u> the entire apartment.

_____

7. (future perfect) They <u>invite</u> more people than they have space for.

_____

8. (past perfect) Fortunately, we <u>adjust</u> the insurance before the accident happened.

_____

9. (present perfect) Surely, he <u>retire</u> by now.

_____

10. (future perfect) His announcement <u>attract</u> a lot of attention.

_____

One of the mildly unusual features of the perfect tenses is that they can be used with both stative and dynamic verbs. The basic meaning of stative verbs, states that continue over time, is a perfect match for the ongoing nature of the perfect tenses. Here are the three perfect tenses with examples of both stative and dynamic verbs:

Present perfect
Stative   John <u>has been</u> a good friend.
Dynamic   John <u>has signed</u> the agreement.

Past perfect
Stative   John <u>had been</u> in graduate school at the time.
Dynamic   John <u>had majored</u> in accounting before he
                      switched to music.

Future perfect
Stative   John <u>will have been</u> at the airport for hours.
Dynamic   John's plane <u>will have landed</u> by now.

The present perfect tense

The present perfect tense consists of a present tense form of the helping verb *have* followed by a verb in the past participle form; for example:

> He <u>has been</u> out sick all week.
> The business <u>has expanded</u> steadily for the past several years.
> I think that I <u>have guessed</u> the answer.
> <u>Have</u> you <u>seen</u> Harry recently?
> We <u>have had</u> a busy day.
> I've just <u>heard</u> the news.

The present perfect tense is used to talk about past-time events that directly affect the present. Notice that none of the previous examples actually mentions the present moment of time; they do not need to because the linkage to the present moment of time is inherent in the meaning of the present perfect. To confirm that this is the case, note what happens when we use past-time adverbs in the examples; they all become ungrammatical:

> X He <u>has been</u> out sick all last week.
> X The business <u>has expanded</u> steadily several years ago.
> X I think that I <u>have guessed</u> the answer last week.
> X <u>Have</u> you <u>seen</u> Harry yesterday?
> X We <u>have had</u> a busy day last Monday.
> X I've <u>heard</u> the news last week.

We use the present perfect tense in two different ways: the main use of the present perfect is for past-time events that have continued over past time up to the present moment of time. We will call this the **continuous** use of the present perfect.

We also use the present perfect for very recent single past-time events that directly impact the present. We will call this the **noncontinuous** use of the present perfect. We will discuss the noncontinuous use of the present perfect after we have discussed the more frequent continuous use.

The continuous use of the present perfect

Here are some examples of the continuous present perfect:

My parents <u>have lived</u> in their house for 30 years.
I <u>have worked</u> there for two years.
She <u>has delivered</u> papers at many major conferences.
Their company <u>has been</u> in business for more than 100 years.
He <u>has owned</u> that truck for as long as I <u>have known</u> him.
I <u>haven't seen</u> my cousin in years.

As was mentioned in Chapter 5, one of the characteristics of all the perfect tenses is that both stative and dynamic verbs can be used freely in all of them. However, there is a difference in the way that the two types of verbs are used. In the present perfect, stative verbs, because of their inherent meaning of an ongoing state or condition, always are normally used with the meaning of an unbroken span of time up to the present moment. Here are some examples of stative verbs:

I <u>have</u> always <u>disliked</u> broccoli.
Our family <u>has</u> always <u>had</u> dogs.
Americans <u>have</u> always <u>loved</u> happy endings in their movies.
John <u>has been</u> a close friend ever since college.
This project <u>has cost</u> us a small fortune.
We <u>have</u> always <u>wanted</u> to go to Hawaii.

Dynamic verbs, on the other hand, typically describe actions that are necessarily intermittent because they start and stop over a period of time. For example, we can legitimately describe the following sentence as continuous in the very real sense that Sam's voting is an activity that is repeated regularly over time, even though he can vote only when elections are held—every two years.

Sam <u>has voted</u> in every election since he was 18.

In the following sentence, Barbara's actions are continuous in the sense that we can imagine Barbara systematically climbing one peak after another until she has climbed them all.

Barbara <u>has climbed</u> every major peak in the Rockies.

In the next sentence, the speaker's infrequent use of his tuxedo still constitutes an activity that has been performed multiple times up to the present moment.

I <u>have worn</u> my tuxedo only three times in the past 20 years.

Here are some more examples of dynamic verbs used in the continuous present perfect:

The kids have gone to the same camp for the past four years.
Our basement has flooded every spring.
I have always parked on the street when I visit them.
Over the years, hail storms have damaged a lot of crops in the area.
She has directed more than 20 plays in her long career.
Our baseball team has won about half of its games.

EXERCISE

6·1

Determine whether the present perfect sentences that follow show a continuously ongoing state (stative verb) or sustained intermittent action (dynamic verb). The first two are done as examples.

Heavy snow has closed the road a dozen times this winter.

ANSWER: Intermittent action (dynamic)

I have always believed that hard work pays off in the end.

ANSWER: Continuously ongoing state (stative)

1. It has rained a lot this week.

   _____

2. The train has always been on time before.

   _____

3. I have never possessed a good sense of direction.

   _____

4. We have spent a lot of money getting ready for this trip.

   _____

5. Have we covered all the topics that are going to be on the final?

   _____

6. The team has never looked better than it has this season.

   _____

7. That car has passed us half a dozen times in the past hour.

   _____

8. I have always felt that his work was not sufficiently appreciated.

   _____

9. We <u>have lost</u> too many games this season because of poor preparation.

_____

10. We <u>have</u> always <u>eaten</u> there when we are in town.

_____

The noncontinuous use of the present perfect

The present perfect also allows for a noncontinuous or single-event use of the perfect tense. Here are some examples of noncontinuous uses:

> The printer <u>has</u> just <u>run</u> out of ink.
> The meeting <u>has been</u> canceled.
> The committee <u>has demanded</u> a second vote.
> The team <u>has picked</u> a new captain.
> We <u>have found</u> the problem, and we can fix it in a few hours.

As you can see, all of these examples describe a onetime only action or event. There is no continuous state or repeated action across a span of time.

In the noncontinuous use of the present perfect, this single, recently completed, past-time event or action directly and immediately affects the present moment of time. This is in contrast to the normal continuous use of the present perfect, which describes a series of events or actions that span a period of past time up to the present moment. For example, compare the following:

Continuous	There <u>have been</u> a lot of bad accidents on the freeway lately.
Noncontinuous	There <u>has been</u> a bad accident on the freeway.

The first sentence with the continuous use of the present perfect describes a situation in which a number of accidents have occurred on the freeway over a span of time. The second sentence with the noncontinuous use of the present perfect describes a single recent accident on the freeway. Using the noncontinuous present perfect emphasizes that (1) the information about the accident is new (and quite possibly not previously known to the audience) and (2) this information impacts the present situation in some way; in our example, the freeway might be closed for hours.

As we would expect, the noncontinuous present perfect is closely tied to the present moment of time. If we shift the time frame of a noncontinuous present perfect sentence to a more distant point in past time, the sentence becomes ungrammatical. For example, compare the following pairs of sentences:

Present time	Their daughter has just graduated from NYU.
Past time	**X** Their daughter has just graduated from NYU last week.
Present time	I've just read your letter.
Past time	**X** I've just read your letter last night.
Present time	We have enjoyed meeting your family.
Past time	**X** We have enjoyed meeting your family yesterday.

In all these examples, the use of the noncontinuous present perfect is totally incompatible with a past-time adverb.

EXERCISE 6·2

Label the underlined present participle verb form as either continuous or noncontinuous. The first two sentences are done as examples:

The Chinese and Americans have argued about trade policies for years.

ANSWER: Continuous

The Chinese and the Americans have agreed on a new trade policy.

ANSWER: Noncontinuous

1. The company has replaced the branch manager.

   _____

2. We have seen several of his plays on Broadway.

   _____

3. He has certainly put on some weight since the last time I saw him.

   _____

4. The conference has arranged transportation for you.

   _____

5. I've found the reference I had been looking for.

   _____

6. I see that they have built an outdoor pool.

   _____

7. We <u>have paid</u> by credit card before whenever we have stayed here.

   _____

8. Wages <u>have increased</u> about 3 percent a year for the past 20 years.

   _____

9. They <u>have</u> finally <u>made</u> up their minds.

   _____

10. We <u>have</u> always <u>used</u> premium gas in that car.

   _____

To understand the meaning and function of the noncontinuous use of the present perfect, we need to contrast it with its alternative: the past tense. In many cases the noncontinuous present perfect and the past tense are interchangeable from a strictly grammatical point of view. For example, we can use the noncontinuous present perfect or the past tense equally well in the following sentences:

Present perfect	There <u>has been</u> a mistake on my income tax.
Past tense	There <u>was</u> a mistake on my income tax.
Present perfect	I've <u>seen</u> the final report.
Past tense	I <u>saw</u> the final report.
Present perfect	Elvis <u>has left</u> the building.
Past tense	Elvis <u>left</u> the building.

However, the implications of the noncontinuous and the past tenses can be quite different.

As we saw in Chapter 3, the past tense is used for events, conditions, or states that are now over and done with. To illustrate this point we used this example:

Samantha <u>went</u> to school at Berkeley.

The sentence not only tells us where Samantha went to school, but the use of the past tense also tells us that Samantha is no longer going to school there. The key point in understanding the difference between the noncontinuous present perfect tense and the past tense is that the past tense erects a wall between past-time events (even ones that occurred in the immediate past) and the present moment of time.

The noncontinuous present perfect, on the other hand, highlights the connection between an event in the immediate and the present moment of time. Often we use the noncontinuous present perfect to emphasize that the past-time information is new to the audience and that the information is of immediate relevance to the present moment. The following pair of sentences is a good illustration of the differences between the noncontinuous present perfect and the past tense:

| Present perfect | I've lost my car keys. |
| Past tense | I lost my car keys. |

Both sentences mean the same thing. However, the present perfect sentence implies (1) that the fact that the speaker lost the keys is new information to the audience and (2) that it is important to the present moment of time. In other words, we all need to help the speaker look for the missing car keys. The past tense is simply a neutral statement of fact about something that happened in the past. There is no necessary implication that this is new information or that the listeners should do anything about it.

Using the noncontinuous present perfect rather than the past tense is a way of telling the audience that what we are saying is new and worth paying attention to. In this sense, it is a kind of emphatic form we might choose over the more standard and expected past tense. For this reason we are more likely to use the noncontinuous present perfect in casual conversation than in writing.

EXERCISE
6·3

Determine whether the underlined verb tense is emphatic (that is, the verb tense emphasizes new and important information) or neutral (that is, the verb tense is a statement of fact). The first two sentences are done as examples.

We have fixed the problem.

ANSWER: Emphatic

We fixed the problem.

ANSWER: Neutral

1. I've got an idea.

_____

2. We made a wrong turn.

_____

3. The witness has admitted mistaking the date of the accident.

_____

4. It has encouraged me to try again.

_____

5. The electricity went out.

_____

6. John <u>has insisted</u> on meeting with the board.

_____

7. I <u>twisted</u> my ankle playing soccer with the kids.

_____

8. We'<u>ve</u> just <u>got</u> an e-mail from the head office.

_____

9. The news <u>surprised</u> everyone.

_____

10. We'<u>ve decided</u> to host a party for their anniversary.

_____

EXERCISE
6·4

Rewrite the underlined verb using both emphatic and neutral tenses. If it is emphatic, use the noncontinuous present perfect tense; if it is neutral, use the past tense. The first sentence is done as an example.

The senator <u>claim</u> that he was misquoted.

EMPHATIC: The senator <u>has claimed</u> that he was misquoted.

NEUTRAL: The senator <u>claimed</u> that he was misquoted.

1. The senator <u>refuse</u> to retract his statement.

Emphatic: _____

Neutral: _____

2. A big tree <u>fall</u> in the backyard.

Emphatic: _____

Neutral: _____

3. A reporter <u>reveal</u> the source of the money.

Emphatic: _____

Neutral: _____

4. They tell me what happened.

Emphatic: _____

Neutral: _____

5. I <u>turn</u> down the offer.

Emphatic: _____

Neutral: _____

6. We <u>buy</u> a new car.

Emphatic: _____

Neutral: _____

7. I <u>find</u> my car keys.

Emphatic: _____

Neutral: _____

8. The CEO <u>saw</u> the new sales figures.

Emphatic: _____

Neutral: _____

9. Our flight <u>be</u> canceled.

Emphatic: _____

Neutral: _____

10. The game <u>end</u> in a tie.

Emphatic: _____

Neutral: _____

The same distinction between the noncontinuous present perfect and past tenses carries over into questions. However, in questions the difference in implications between the noncontinuous present perfect and past tenses can be more significant, sometimes even amounting to a shift in meaning. For example, compare the noncontinuous present perfect and past tense versions of the same question:

Present perfect tense	Have you <u>seen</u> the play at the Civic Theater?
Past tense	Did you <u>see</u> the play at the Civic Theater?

The noncontinuous present perfect with its present-time relevancy implies (among other things) that the play is still running at the Civic Theater and the person being addressed still has a chance to see it if he or she hasn't done so already. The past tense in the second sentence definitely implies that the play's run is over and that the person being addressed has no further opportunity to see the play even if he or she wanted to.

The previous pair of sentences is a dramatic example of how distinct the implications of questions in the noncontinuous present perfect and past tenses can be. The difference between them is usually more modest. Here is a typical example:

Present perfect tense	Have you <u>reported</u> the accident to the police?
Past tense	<u>Did</u> you <u>report</u> the accident to the police?

The first question with the noncontinuous present perfect tense reflects a built-in expectation that reporting an accident to the police is something that people would normally do. Thus, asking the question in the present perfect conveys a tacit expectation that the answer would be "yes." The past tense question, on the other hand, is much more neutral. The past tense question does not voice the same expectation about reporting the accident to the police. It is a simple, factual question without the built-in positive implications of the noncontinuous present perfect question.

Here is a second example:

Present perfect tense	Have you <u>ordered</u> the pizza?
Past tense	<u>Did</u> you <u>order</u> the pizza?

The two questions have the same basic meaning. The differences in implication, however, are substantial. The first question with the noncontinuous present perfect tense implies that there was a definite plan to order pizza. The question functions as a confirmation of the fact that the pizza has already been ordered as expected: the person asking this question anticipates either of two possible answers: "yes" or "not yet."

The past tense question is much more neutral. Maybe the person ordered the pizza or maybe not—either answer is equally plausible. The use of the past tense is more like a genuine open-ended question than the present perfect version.

EXERCISE
6·5

Decide whether the following questions have affirmative or neutral expectations. The first two are done as examples.

<u>Have</u> you just <u>got</u> here?

ANSWER: Affirmative expectation

<u>Did</u> you just <u>get</u> here?

ANSWER: Neutral expectation

1. Did they find out how the fire started?

_____

2. Has the medication helped relieve the pain?

_____

3. Have you met everyone?

_____

4. Did the plumber finally show up?

_____

5. Has the jury reached a verdict?

_____

6. Did they grow these vegetables themselves?

_____

7. Did you remember to walk the dog before you left?

_____

8. Have you learned anything from this experience?

_____

9. Have they decided what they are going to do?

_____

10. Did you drive to work this morning?

_____

Turn the following statements into questions with both affirmative and neutral expectations. If the question has an affirmative expectation, use the noncontinuous present perfect tense. If the question has a neutral expectation, use the past tense. The first sentence is done as an example.

They replied to the e-mail.

ANSWER: Affirmative expectation: Have they replied to the e-mail?

NEUTRAL: Did they reply to the e-mail?

1. The Coast Guard <u>warned</u> boaters about the storm.

   Affirmative expectation: _____

   Neutral: _____

2. The paint <u>dried</u>.

   Affirmative expectation: _____

   Neutral: _____

3. The committee <u>adopted</u> the proposal.

   Affirmative expectation: _____

   Neutral: _____

4. He <u>buy</u> the tickets.

   Affirmative expectation: _____

   Neutral: _____

5. The garage <u>checked</u> the battery.

   Affirmative expectation: _____

   Neutral: _____

6. You <u>stayed</u> there before.

   Affirmative expectation: _____

   Neutral: _____

7. She <u>kept</u> the receipts.

   Affirmative expectation: _____

   Neutral: _____

8. They <u>responded</u> to our offer.

   Affirmative expectation: _____

   Neutral: _____

9. You <u>get</u> enough to eat.

   Affirmative expectation: _____

   Neutral: _____

10. They <u>started</u> to work.

    Affirmative expectation: _____

    Neutral: _____

The past perfect tense

The past perfect tense consists of the helping verb *had* (the past tense of *have*) followed by a verb in the past participle form. Here are some examples:

> I called her, but she <u>had</u> already <u>left</u> for the day.
> The passes were all closed because we <u>had had</u> so much snow.
> The caller <u>had</u> already <u>hung</u> up by the time I answered the phone.
> I told him that I <u>had</u> already <u>made</u> up my mind.
> They bought an old house that <u>had been</u> built in the 1920s.

Time, the old joke goes, was invented to keep everything from happening all at once. Likewise, the past perfect tense was invented to keep two different past-time events from happening all at once. For this reason, the past perfect tense is sometimes called "the past in the past."

The two past-time events are almost always clauses—usually an independent clause and a subordinate clause, but sometimes two independent clauses. The clause in the past perfect tense describes an action or event that has been completed before the action or event in the clause in the past tense takes place. Here are some examples of both types of clauses:

Independent clause and subordinate clause
(Note that some types of independent and subordinate clauses can be in either order. That is, the clause with the past perfect tense can either precede or follow the past tense clause.)

> They sold the house after they <u>had remodeled</u> it extensively.
>   more recent past-time event   older past-time event

> I <u>had</u> just <u>stepped</u> into the shower when the phone rang.
>   older past-time event   more recent past-time event

> We got a new rug because the old one <u>had faded</u> so badly.
>   more recent past-time event   older past-time event

> The landscapers removed the trees that <u>had grown</u> too big.
>   more recent past-time event   older past-time event

Two independent clauses

They asked us to go with them, but we <u>had</u> already <u>made</u> other plans.
        more recent past-time event   older past-time event

I wanted to get a ride with Jim, but he <u>had</u> already <u>left</u>.
     more recent past-time event   older past-time event

EXERCISE
7·1

Each of the following sentences contains two past-time clauses. Underline the past perfect tense. Then label the older clause as "older past-time event" and the newer one as "more recent past-time event." The first two sentences are done as examples.

We asked them to redo the tests that had been done last week.

ANSWER: We asked them to redo the tests that <u>had been done</u> last week.
        more recent past-time event   older past-time event

We went for a drive as soon as we had finished washing the car.

ANSWER: We went for a drive as soon as we <u>had finished</u> washing the car.
        more recent past-time event   older past-time event

1. We revised the estimates that we had made earlier.

2. He went into the hospital after his temperature had reached 103 degrees.

3. They had patented the device before they put it on the market.

4. I tried to get tickets, but they had already sold out.

5. We fell into bed utterly exhausted as soon as we had eaten.

6. The sun came out for the first time in days after the storm had finally passed.

7. I knew the answer as soon as she had asked the question.

8. I had picked up a cold when I was traveling.

9. We had lived there some time before we met them.

10. The bakery stopped making the cake that everyone had liked so much.

The meaning and use of the past perfect tense is quite straightforward. The main difficulty using the past perfect tense is with sentences that contain an independent clause and an adverb clause because adverb clauses, unlike other types of clauses, can be moved around, making it more difficult to determine which clause should be in the past perfect tense and which should be in the past tense. Accordingly, we will focus the remaining discussion of the past perfect tense on sentences containing an independent clause and an adverb subordinate clause.

Let us begin by looking closely at an example of a sentence with an adverb clause:

I <u>had been</u> an intern for two years before they made me a job offer.
   main clause   adverb clause

The past perfect portion of the sentence in the main clause expresses the older time—the two-year period that the speaker was an intern. The past tense portion of the sentence in the adverb clause expresses a second, more recent event—the speaker's being offered a job. The whole point of using the past perfect tense is to separate this sentence, all of which takes place in the past, into two distinct past-time frames—the older time period of the internship and the more recent event of the job offer. The use of the two different tenses enables us to place the two past-time events into a clear and unequivocal chronological sequence.

Sometimes the time sequencing imposed by the two different tenses can even imply a cause and effect relationship between the two clauses. For example:

They <u>had had</u> a big fight just before they broke up.
   main clause   adverb clause

This sequencing leads us to think that their fight may have caused their subsequent breakup.

Adverb clauses are dependent clauses that play the role of adverbs. As with single-word adverbs, adverb clauses modify verbs by giving more information about the time, place, manner, or cause of the action of the verb. Here we are concerned only with adverb clauses that give information about time or (occasionally) cause.

In our first set of examples of past perfect tenses in adverb clauses, all of the past perfect tenses will be in the main clause:

The driver <u>had suffered</u> a heart attack before the car ran off the road.
   main clause   adverb clause

The plane <u>had been</u> airborne for about two hours when the left engine quit.
   main clause   adverb clause

He <u>had committed</u> himself to the plan before he knew all the facts.
   main clause   adverb clause

We <u>had repainted</u> the house before we put it on the market.
   main clause   adverb clause

One of the characteristics of adverb clauses is that they can be moved from their normal position following the main clause to a position in front of the main clause. (When we move the adverb clause in front of the main clause, the adverb clause is said to be **inverted**.)

We must separate the inverted introductory adverb clause from the main clause by a comma. (We do not use a comma to separate the main clause from the adverb clause when the adverb clause is in a position following the main clause.) Here are the previous example sentences now with the adverb clauses in inverted positions:

Before the car ran off the road, the driver <u>had suffered</u> a heart attack.
  adverb clause   main clause

When the left engine quit, the plane <u>had been</u> airborne for about two hours.
  adverb clause   main clause

Before he knew all the facts, he <u>had committed</u> himself to the plan.
  adverb clause   main clause

Before we put it on the market, we <u>had repainted</u> the house.
  adverb clause   main clause

Inverting adverb clauses has no effect on the grammatical meaning of the sentence. The only difference is in emphasis: putting the adverb clause first gives it greater relative emphasis following the general rhetorical principle that any grammatical structure moved out of its normal position (especially when it is moved to the first position in the sentence) automatically becomes more prominent.

EXERCISE

7·2

All of the following sentences contain a main clause in the past perfect tense followed by an adverb clause in the past tense. Invert the two clauses so that the adverb clause is given greater emphasis. Be sure to use a comma with the inverted adverb clause. The first sentence is done as an example.

It <u>had stopped</u> snowing by the time we got to airport.

ANSWER: By the time we got to the airport, it <u>had stopped</u> snowing.

1. We <u>had adjusted</u> the car seats before we started driving.

  _____

2. The waiter <u>had started</u> clearing the dishes before everyone finished eating.

  _____

3. The ice cream <u>had</u> already <u>melted</u> by the time we cut the cake.

  _____

4. The house <u>had been</u> empty for years when we first moved in.

  _____

5. We <u>had</u> already <u>finished</u> setting the table before I noticed the dirty glasses.

_____

6. He <u>had advertised</u> the job opening before the position was approved.

_____

7. The sun <u>had risen</u> long before we got on the road.

_____

8. The rebels <u>had</u> already <u>abandoned</u> the fort before the soldiers arrived.

_____

9. The rain <u>had stopped</u> by the time we got our tents set up.

_____

10. I <u>had heard</u> the loud music even before I reached the door.

_____

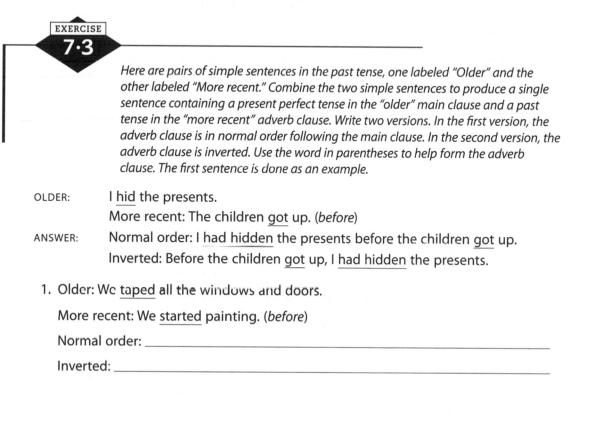

EXERCISE
7·3

Here are pairs of simple sentences in the past tense, one labeled "Older" and the other labeled "More recent." Combine the two simple sentences to produce a single sentence containing a present perfect tense in the "older" main clause and a past tense in the "more recent" adverb clause. Write two versions. In the first version, the adverb clause is in normal order following the main clause. In the second version, the adverb clause is inverted. Use the word in parentheses to help form the adverb clause. The first sentence is done as an example.

OLDER: I <u>hid</u> the presents.
           More recent: The children <u>got</u> up. _(before)_

ANSWER: Normal order: I <u>had hidden</u> the presents before the children <u>got</u> up.
           Inverted: Before the children <u>got</u> up, I <u>had hidden</u> the presents.

1. Older: We <u>taped</u> all the windows and doors.

   More recent: We <u>started</u> painting. _(before)_

   Normal order: _____

   Inverted: _____

2. Older: John already <u>swam</u> competitively.

   More recent: He <u>went</u> to college. (*before*)

   Normal order: _____

   Inverted: _____

3. Older: Everyone <u>put</u> on protective headgear.

   More recent: They <u>went</u> bicycle riding. (*before*)

   Normal order: _____

   Inverted: _____

4. Older: I <u>skipped</u> lunch.

   More recent: I <u>had</u> an important conference call at noon. (*because*)

   Normal order: _____

   Inverted: _____

5. Older: The lawyers totally <u>revised</u> their strategy.

   More recent: The court <u>reconvened</u> after lunch. (*before*)

   Normal order: _____

   Inverted: _____

6. Older: The cook <u>rubbed</u> the roast with herbs.

   More recent: He <u>put</u> it in the oven. (*before*)

   Normal order: _____

   Inverted: _____

7. Older: He <u>hesitated</u> noticeably.

   More recent: He <u>answered</u> the question. (*before*)

   Normal order: _____

   Inverted: _____

8. Older: They <u>drained</u> a lot of water out of the reservoir.

   More recent: The heavy rains <u>came</u>. (*before*)

   Normal order: _____

   Inverted: _____

9. Older: The company <u>analyzed</u> the proposal carefully.

More recent: They <u>invested</u> money in it. (*before*)

Normal order: _____

Inverted: _____

10. Older: They <u>got</u> extra car insurance.

More recent: Their son <u>was</u> old enough to drive. (*as soon as*)

Normal order: _____

Inverted: _____

To this point all of our examples of past perfect tenses used in sentences with adverb clauses have had the past perfect verb in the main clause. However, the past perfect verb is actually more often used in the adverb clause. Here are some examples:

We cleared off the driveway as soon as it <u>had stopped</u> snowing.
    main clause   adverb clause

My bicycle got a flat tire before we <u>had gone</u> two miles.
    main clause   adverb clause

I wasn't able to play because I <u>had injured</u> my leg last week.
    main clause   adverb clause

The janitor always locked the gym up after the team buses <u>had departed</u>.
    main clause   adverb clause

These adverb clauses can also be inverted, putting the past perfect verb in the first clause:

As soon as it <u>had stopped</u> snowing, we cleared off the driveway.
    adverb clause   main clause

Before we <u>had gone</u> two miles, my bicycle got a flat tire.
    adverb clause   main clause

Because I <u>had injured</u> my leg last week, I wasn't able to play.
    adverb clause   main clause

After the team buses <u>had departed</u>, the janitor always locked the gym up.
    adverb clause   main clause

All of the following sentences contain a main clause in the past tense followed by an adverb clause in the past perfect tense. Invert the two clauses so that the adverb clause is given greater emphasis. Be sure to use a comma with the inverted adverb. The first sentence is done as an example:

I knew my wallet was on the dresser because I <u>had put</u> it there the night before.

ANSWER: Because I <u>had put</u> it there the night before, I knew my wallet was on the dresser.

1. I called them on my cell phone as soon as the plane <u>had landed</u>.

   _____

2. I knew the answer even before he <u>had finished</u> asking me the question.

   _____

3. Our team scored even before we <u>had found</u> our seats.

   _____

4. We hung the clothes on the line after the sun <u>had come</u> out.

   _____

5. We could declare a thesis topic after we <u>had passed</u> the qualifying exam.

   _____

6. I had to come up with a plan even before we'd <u>had</u> a chance to talk about it.

   _____

7. We looked for better seats after we <u>had reboarded</u> the bus.

   _____

8. General Lee became a college president after the Civil War <u>had ended</u>.

   _____

9. It functioned much better after they <u>had repaired</u> it.

_____

10. The plane finally took off after we <u>had sat</u> on the tarmac for an hour.

_____

Here are pairs of simple sentences in the past tense, one labeled "More recent" and the other labeled "Older." Combine the two simple sentences to produce a single sentence containing a past tense in the "more recent" main clause and a present perfect tense in the "older" adverb clause. Write two versions. In the first version, the adverb clause is in normal order following the main clause. In the second version, the adverb clause is inverted. The first sentence is done as an example. (Your answers may have slightly different wording.)

MORE RECENT: Bob <u>was</u> able to play again. (main clause)

OLDER: He <u>had</u> surgery on his injured knee. (adverb clause)

ANSWER: Normal order: Bob <u>was</u> able to play again after he <u>had had</u> surgery on his injured knee.

INVERTED: After he <u>had had</u> surgery on his injured knee, Bob <u>was</u> able to play again.

1. More recent: They <u>were</u> eligible to play professional football. (main clause)

   Older: Their class <u>graduated</u> from college. (adverb clause)

   Normal order: _____

   Inverted: _____

2. More recent: The airlines <u>instituted</u> a new policy. (main clause)

   Older: There <u>was</u> a near collision on the tarmac. (adverb clause)

   Normal order: _____

   Inverted: _____

3. More recent: He <u>was</u> arrested. (main clause)

   Older: He <u>lied</u> to the grand jury under oath. (adverb clause)

   Normal order: _____

   Inverted: _____

4. More recent: Ralph quit his job and moved to Florida. (main clause)

   Older: Ralph won the lottery. (adverb clause)

   Normal order: _____

   Inverted: _____

5. More recent: The cloth shrunk badly. (main clause)

   Older: The cloth got wet. (adverb clause)

   Normal order: _____

   Inverted: _____

6. More recent: The protesters were arrested. (main clause)

   Older: The protesters disrupted a city council meeting. (adverb clause)

   Normal order: _____

   Inverted: _____

7. More recent: The witness was excused from testifying. (main clause)

   Older: The witness invoked her right against self-incrimination. (adverb clause)

   Normal order: _____

   Inverted: _____

8. More recent: Someone called the fire department. (main clause)

   Older: The residents were alerted by the smell of smoke. (adverb clause)

   Normal order: _____

   Inverted: _____

9. More recent: The meetings were better attended. (main clause)

   Older: They started serving refreshments. (adverb clause)

   Normal order: _____

   Inverted: _____

10. More recent: The dog chewed up all the furniture. (main clause)

    Older: They left for work that morning. (adverb clause)

    Normal order: _____

    Inverted: _____

Summary of sentences with adverb clauses

Using the past perfect tenses with sentences that contain adverb clauses is confusing for two reasons: (1) adverb clauses can be either in their normal positions after main clauses or they can be inverted, and (2) it is quite common for the past perfect tense to be used in the main clause rather than the adverb clause. Thus, there are no fewer than four possibilities for where the past perfect tense can occur:

- The past perfect tense is in a main clause in its normal initial position.
  Example: We <u>had packed</u> a picnic lunch before we left.
          main clause   adverb clause
- The past perfect tense is in a main clause, but the main clause is in the second position following an inverted adverb clause.
  Example: Before we left, we <u>had packed</u> a picnic lunch.
- The past perfect tense is in the adverb clause in its normal position following the main clause.
  Example: It took a while to clean the pot because the rice <u>had boiled</u> over.
- The past perfect tense is in an adverb clause inverted to a position in front of the main clause.
  Example: Because the rice <u>had boiled</u> over, it took a while to clean the pot.

The future perfect tense

The future perfect tense verb form consists of *will have* (the future tense form of *have*) followed by a verb in the past perfect form. Here are some examples:

> By then, everyone <u>will have finished</u> eating.
> The office <u>will have closed</u> before we can get there.
> They <u>will have lived</u> in Japan for six years this coming January.

The future perfect tense, as all of the perfect tenses, must be terminated or "perfected" by an even more distant moment of time or defining event. In the case of the future perfect tense, this more distant moment is defined by an adverb prepositional phrase (usually beginning with the preposition *by*) or by an adverb clause of time. Here are some examples:

Terminating adverb prepositional phrase
The moon <u>will have set</u> by midnight.
The team <u>will have come</u> out onto the field by now.
Amazon <u>will have shipped</u> our order by the end of next week.

Terminating adverb clause of time
They <u>will have rented</u> a place to stay before school starts in the fall.
He <u>will have figured</u> out the answer as soon as he gets all the clues.
The chairman <u>will have replaced Harry</u> before the board meets on
   Monday.

The future perfect tense is used to talk about future-time events or conditions that will be completed or concluded no later than some specified future time or future event; for example:

Specified future time
I <u>will have entered</u> all the data before the end of the day.
The kitchen <u>will have stopped</u> serving by 10:00.
I <u>will have earned</u> $5,000 by the end of the summer.
The storm <u>will have blocked</u> all the roads by nightfall.

Specified future event

The painters <u>will have finished</u> the interior before the carpets are laid.

We <u>will have paid</u> the developers a fortune by the time we are finished.

They <u>will have gotten</u> the tents up before it starts raining.

I <u>will have graded</u> the papers before class begins.

When we talk about future conditions, we often use stative verbs with an adverb of duration; for example:

> They <u>will have been</u> married <u>for 10 years</u> this June.
>   adverb of duration

> I <u>will have owned</u> my truck <u>for two years</u> this coming Labor Day.
>   adverb of duration

> I <u>will have had</u> a cold <u>for two weeks</u> now.
>   adverb of duration

The difference between the future tense and the future perfect tense is that the future perfect tense is used to emphasize the completion of the future event. For example, compare the following sentences:

Future tense	We <u>will have</u> dinner by 7:00.
Future perfect tense	We <u>will have had</u> dinner by 7:00.

The future tense sentence implies that dinner will start by 7:00. The future perfect tense implies that dinner will be over by 7:00.

Here is another example:

Future tense	The clouds <u>will break</u> up by noon.
Future perfect tense	The clouds <u>will have broken</u> up by noon.

The future tense sentence implies that we will have at least partial sun by noon. The future perfect sentence implies that the clouds will be completely gone by noon.

Here is an example where the difference is more subtle:

Future tense	Larry <u>will get</u> to the office around 9:00.
Future perfect tense	Larry <u>will have gotten</u> to the office around 9:00.

The sentence with the future tense envisions Larry arriving at the office at or before 9:00. The sentence with the future perfect tense envisions that at or before 9:00, Larry will already have been settled in his office for some time.

In general, we can say that the future tense envisions a future event happening. The future perfect tense envisions that future event as already being completed.

Rewrite the underlined infinitive verbs either as future tenses or future perfect tenses depending on how the sentence is labeled. If it is labeled "Happening," use the future tense. If it is labeled "Completed," use the future perfect. The first two sentences are done as examples.

Completed: All of the flights <u>be</u> grounded by the storm as of 10 p.m.

ANSWER: All of the flights <u>will have been</u> grounded by the storm as of 10 p.m.

Happening: The stock market <u>collapse</u> by the end of the year.

ANSWER: The stock market <u>will collapse</u> by the end of the year.

1. Completed: The two companies <u>merge</u> by the end of the fiscal year.

   _____

2. Happening: I think that they <u>make</u> me an offer soon.

   _____

3. Completed: They <u>trace</u> the source of the leak in a few hours.

   _____

4. Happening: The carpets <u>fade</u> quickly if they are not protected from the sun.

   _____

5. Completed: Surely any message they sent <u>reach</u> us by now.

   _____

6. Completed: Hurry, or they <u>sell</u> all the good seats by the time we get our orders in.

   _____

7. Happening: The doctor <u>prescribe</u> a different medication after seeing what happened.

   _____

8. Completed: Her heirs <u>gain</u> control of their estate when they turned 18.

   _____

9. Completed: The chair <u>cut</u> off discussion after two hours.

   _____

10. Completed: The police <u>inform</u> him of his rights the moment he was arrested.

   _____

Introduction to the progressive tenses

·9·

There are three progressive tenses: the **present progressive**, the **past progressive**, and the **future progressive**. The three progressive tenses are all formed in exactly parallel manner: the appropriate present, past, or future tense form of the helping verb *be* followed by a verb in the present participle form; for example:

Present progressive	They <u>are working</u> in the garden now.
Past progressive	They <u>were working</u> in the garden earlier.
Future progressive	They <u>will be working</u> in the garden this afternoon.

The basic meaning of the progressive tense is an action in progress (thus the name **progressive** tense) at a particular moment in time. The present progressive is an action in progress at the present moment or period of time. The past progressive is an action in progress at some moment or period in the past. The future progressive is an action in progress at some moment or period in the future.

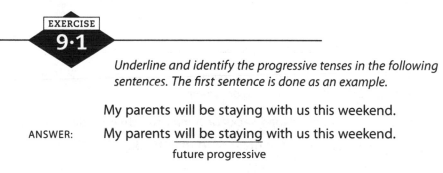

EXERCISE
9·1

Underline and identify the progressive tenses in the following sentences. The first sentence is done as an example.

My parents will be staying with us this weekend.

ANSWER: My parents <u>will be staying</u> with us this weekend.
future progressive

1. Our company is sponsoring a number of charity auctions.

_____

2. We were just admiring your garden.

_____

3. Our pets will be going to the vet for their annual shots.

_____

4. I am translating some technical manuals into Spanish.

_____

5. The kids will be staying overnight at a friend's house.

_____

6. Am I interrupting anything?

_____

7. They will be completing their training in June.

_____

8. I was falling asleep at my desk so I took a little walk to wake up.

_____

9. I don't know why they are blaming me for what happened.

_____

10. Remember, they will be relying on you.

_____

Replace the underlined verb with the progressive verb form identified in parentheses. The first sentence is done as an example.

(past progressive) The farmers <u>load</u> sacks of grain onto their trucks.

ANSWER: The farmers <u>were loading</u> sacks of grain onto their trucks.

1. (future progressive) You <u>waste</u> your time if you do that.

_____

2. (present progressive) I <u>make</u> some coffee; would you like some?

_____

3. (past progressive) The polls <u>lean</u> toward the incumbent candidate.

_____

4. (future progressive) I <u>teach</u> part-time next year.

_____

5. (past progressive) The heat <u>kill</u> all of our shade plants.

_____

6. (future progressive) Their flight <u>arrive</u> at 9:45.

_____

7. (present progressive) They <u>refer</u> the whole matter to their legal department.

_____

8. (past progressive) I thought that they <u>deal</u> with the situation very well.

_____

9. (future progressive) We <u>discuss</u> that issue at our next meeting.

_____

10. (present progressive) His doctor <u>treat</u> the infection with a new antibiotic.

_____

The present progressive tense

The present progressive tense consists of the helping verb *be* in a present tense form followed by a verb in the present participle *-ing* form. Here are some examples:

> Our builder is leasing some heavy equipment to clear the site.
> The heavy rain is washing ruts into our front yard.
> I am telephoning all of the committee members.
> We are going to my parents' home for Christmas.
> It seems that traffic is getting worse every month.
> I'm hoping that I could see you for a few minutes this afternoon.
> He is always coming in late to meetings.

The present progressive tense has two main meanings: (1) action in progress and (2) future. In addition, there are two idiomatic uses of the present progressive that we will discuss at the end of the chapter.

Using the present progressive for action in progress

"Action in progress" accounts for around 80 percent of the occurrences of the present progressive. The term *action in progress* refers to the fact that we use the present progressive tense to narrate or depict an action or event that takes place or "progresses" (hence the name of the tense "progressive") over some span of current time. What constitutes "some span of current time" is very broad.

The action can take place during the actual time of speaking; for example:

> I'm just calling to say hello.
> The children are opening their presents even as we speak.

Or, the action can take place over great periods of time; for example:

> The Pacific plate is slowly diving under the North American plate.
> The two galaxies are passing through each other over a period of millennia.

On the face of it, the present progressive tense in the sense of "action in progress" seems perfectly straightforward. In many ways it is, but it is surprisingly difficult for nonnative speakers to use correctly. In fact, advanced nonnative speakers of English probably make more errors with this meaning of the present progressive tense than with any other single verb form in English.

The problem is not in forming the present progressive correctly or in using it in appropriate situations. The main problem is that there are some aspects of the progressive tenses (the present progressive in particular) that lead nonnative speakers to use the present progressive tense with stative verbs, verbs that are incompatible with the progressive tenses.

There are two important areas of differences between dynamic verbs and stative verbs that are especially relevant to the progressive tenses: the nature of subject-verb relationships and how the two types of verbs treat time.

Subject-verb relationships

Dynamic and stative verbs enter into very different relationships with their subjects. Dynamic verbs require the subject to be the performer or "doer" of the action of the verb. For example:

> Frank answered the phone.
> Janet taught English in China for a few years.
> Farmer Brown planted potatoes this year.

In these dynamic verb sentences, the subjects are the performers of the action of the verbs: Frank performed the action of answering the phone; Janet performed the action of teaching English; Farmer Brown performed the action of planting potatoes.

Stative verbs enter into a different kind of relationship with their subjects, describing the ongoing condition or state of their subjects; for example:

> Frank has a cell phone but no landline.
> Janet knows a lot about teaching English in China.
> Farmer Brown owns 500 acres of land in Idaho.

None of the subjects in these examples are doing anything. Instead, the verbs are describing something about the nature or situation of the subjects: Frank's ownership of telephones is described; Janet is described as knowing a lot about teaching English in China; and Farmer Brown is described as owning land in Idaho (where he can grow his potatoes).

Sometimes, especially with mental or cognitive verbs, the subject-verb difference between stative and dynamic verbs is not obvious at first glance. Compare the following two sentences:

> Betty figured out the answer to the question.
> Betty knew the answer to the question.

Often with mental or cognitive verbs the difference between stative and dynamic comes down to this question: Is the subject intentionally performing the action of the verb? In the first example, Betty has actively engaged in the process of coming up with the answer to the question. The solution came about only because Betty intentionally made it happen. The second example is different. We don't necessarily choose to know things. For example, all of us have the lyrics to hundreds of idiotic pop songs from our teenage years cluttering up our brains. We would all be happy to get rid of these lyrics to free up more mental storage space if only we could.

Figure (out) is thus a dynamic verb, and *know* is thus a stative verb. When we use the two verbs in the present progressive, we see the difference in grammaticality:

> Betty is figuring out the answer to the question.
> **X** Betty is knowing the answer to the question.

Another challenge is that many verbs can be either stative or dynamic verbs depending on the way they are used. For example, the verb *appear* can be used as either a dynamic verb or a stative verb (note that both are grammatical in the past tense):

> *Dynamic verb*   Jerome appeared in a Hollywood film.
> *Stative verb*   Jerome appeared to be a little distracted.

In the dynamic verb sentence, *appear* means "play a role." In the stative verb sentence, *appear* means "seem to other people." As we would expect, the dynamic verb use is grammatical in the present progressive tense, while the stative verb use is not:

> *Dynamic verb*   Jerome is appearing in a Hollywood film.
> *Stative verb*   **X** Jerome is appearing to be a little distracted.

In the dynamic verb sentence, the subject *Jerome* is an agent performing the action of the verb *appear*. In the stative verb sentence, the same subject is not doing anything. Instead, the sentence comments on how the subject *Jerome* seems to other people.

EXERCISE
10·1

Each of the following items has two sentences, one with a stative verb and one with a dynamic verb. Relying solely on the relationship between the subject and the verb, identify which verb is the stative verb and which is the dynamic verb. The stative verb will describe the nature of the subject; the dynamic verb will carry out the action of the subject. Confirm your answers by using both sentences in the present progressive tense. The first sentence is done as an example.

The children always like to play outside.

The children always ask to play outside.

The children always <u>like</u> to play outside. **Stative**

The children always <u>ask</u> to play outside. **Dynamic**

Present progressive: **X** The children <u>are</u> always <u>liking</u> to play outside.

Present progressive: The children <u>are</u> always <u>asking</u> to play outside.

1. The sausages <u>weigh</u> two pounds.

   The butcher <u>weighs</u> the sausages.

   Present progressive: _____

   Present progressive: _____

2. College graduates <u>pile up</u> a lot of debt.

   College graduates <u>owe</u> a lot of money.

   Present progressive: _____

   Present progressive: _____

3. Bill <u>has</u> a broken toe.

   Bill <u>has</u> some friends over to celebrate his promotion.

   Present progressive: _____

   Present progressive: _____

4. The children <u>appear</u> to be ready to go.

   The situation <u>changes</u> by the minute.

   Present progressive: _____

   Present progressive: _____

5. The kids always <u>turn</u> their bedroom into a playground.

   The kids' bedroom <u>resembles</u> the scene of a natural disaster.

   Present progressive: _____

   Present progressive: _____

6. Her new hairstyle <u>suits</u> her very well.

   Her new hairstyle <u>takes</u> a lot of time to maintain.

   Present progressive: _____

   Present progressive: _____

7. Everyone <u>tells</u> me to be careful.

   Everyone <u>needs</u> to be careful.

   Present progressive: _____

   Present progressive: _____

8. The public <u>doubts</u> what the congressman is claiming.

   The public <u>agrees</u> with what the congressman is claiming.

   Present progressive: _____

   Present progressive: _____

9. A big payment <u>comes</u> due at the end of the month.

   A big problem <u>exists</u> in our cash flow.

   Present progressive: _____

   Present progressive: _____

10. The students <u>discussed</u> how to thank you.

    The students <u>appreciate</u> all that you have done for them.

    Present progressive: _____

    Present progressive: _____

Time

The second major difference between dynamic and stative verbs is how they relate to time. Dynamic verbs are time bound; that is, the action of the verb always takes place in real time. Accordingly, the time of a dynamic verb's action can always be expressed by an adverb of time (either an adverb prepositional phrase or an adverb clause). For example:

> Jennifer <u>bought</u> a leather jacket.

This is a grammatically complete sentence without any overt expression of time. However, because the action of buying a jacket must take place in time, we *always* have the option of adding an adverb of time (either an adverb prepositional phrase or an adverb clause) to specify the time of the action; for example:

> Jennifer <u>bought</u> a leather jacket **last week.** (adverb prepositional phrase)
> Jennifer <u>bought</u> a leather jacket **when she was in Denver.** (adverb clause)

Stative verbs, on the other hand, are not time bound—just the opposite. Stative verbs are not limited at all by time.

Jennifer <u>owns</u> a leather jacket.

In this stative sentence, the stative verb *owns* describes something about the nature or character of the subject (Jennifer). In this case the verb tells us that she has a leather jacket. When somebody owns something, that state of ownership is not time bound. Ownership is an ongoing state with no built-in time limitation. When we own something, we own it indefinitely; we own it until we decide to get rid of it or otherwise lose possession of it.

If we try to modify a stative verb with an adverb of time, we are essentially mixing two incompatible systems: the inherently unlimited time of the stative verb with the limitation of the adverb of time. The result is necessarily both ungrammatical and nonsensical:

X **Jennifer owns a leather jacket at five this afternoon.** (adverb prepositional phrase)
X Jennifer owns a leather jacket **when she goes to dinner.** (adverb clause)

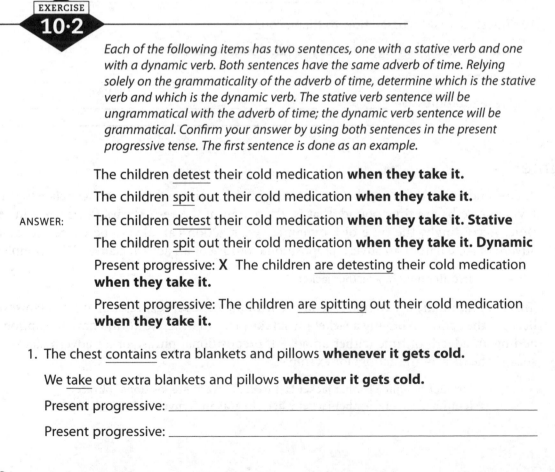

10·2

Each of the following items has two sentences, one with a stative verb and one with a dynamic verb. Both sentences have the same adverb of time. Relying solely on the grammaticality of the adverb of time, determine which is the stative verb and which is the dynamic verb. The stative verb sentence will be ungrammatical with the adverb of time; the dynamic verb sentence will be grammatical. Confirm your answer by using both sentences in the present progressive tense. The first sentence is done as an example.

The children <u>detest</u> their cold medication **when they take it.**

The children <u>spit</u> out their cold medication **when they take it.**

ANSWER: The children <u>detest</u> their cold medication **when they take it. Stative**

The children <u>spit</u> out their cold medication **when they take it. Dynamic**

Present progressive: X The children <u>are detesting</u> their cold medication **when they take it.**

Present progressive: The children <u>are spitting</u> out their cold medication **when they take it.**

1. The chest <u>contains</u> extra blankets and pillows **whenever it gets cold.**

   We <u>take</u> out extra blankets and pillows **whenever it gets cold.**

   Present progressive: _____

   Present progressive: _____

92 PRACTICE MAKES PERFECT English Verb Tenses Up Close

2. I <u>resolved</u> the issue **in a minute.**

   Everyone <u>recognizes</u> the issue **in a minute.**

   Present progressive: _____

   Present progressive: _____

3. We <u>track</u> the paths of protons **when we are in the lab.**

   Atoms <u>consist</u> of protons **when we are in the lab.**

   Present progressive: _____

   Present progressive: _____

4. They <u>seem</u> to be reliable **all the time.**

   We <u>check</u> on their reliability **all the time.**

   Present progressive: _____

   Present progressive: _____

5. He <u>finds</u> out what the answer is **on Wednesday.**

   He <u>understands</u> what the answer is **on Wednesday.**

   Present progressive: _____

   Present progressive: _____

6. The new shoes <u>fit</u> well **every weekend.**

   I <u>wear</u> the new shoes **every weekend.**

   Present progressive: _____

   Present progressive: _____

7. We <u>buy</u> a new car **next week.**

   A new car <u>costs</u> more than we can afford **next week.**

   Present progressive: _____

   Present progressive: _____

8. The children <u>love</u> their new school **in the fall.**

   The children <u>enter</u> their new school **in the fall.**

   Present progressive: _____

   Present progressive: _____

9. Their new apartment <u>looks</u> like their old place **when they move in.**

   They <u>plan</u> to remodel their new apartment **when they move in.**

   Present progressive: _____

   Present progressive: _____

10. Everyone <u>helps</u> to rearrange the layout of our office **every Monday morning.**

    Everyone <u>dislikes</u> the layout of our office **every Monday morning.**

    Present progressive: _____

    Present progressive: _____

Different verb tenses interact with dynamic and stative verbs in different ways. The past tense is unusual in that it is equally accepting of both dynamic and stative verbs; for example:

Dynamic verb	Jennifer <u>bought</u> a leather jacket last week.
Stative verb	Jennifer <u>owned</u> a leather jacket when she lived in Denver.

The fact that the past tense can be freely used with both kinds of verbs is undoubtedly why most novels and other works of fiction are written in the past tense: writers can mix dynamic and stative verbs without problems of grammatical or semantic incompatibility.

The present tense will readily permit stative verbs but not dynamic verbs unless they are used in special ways; for example:

Stative verb	Jennifer <u>owns</u> a leather jacket.
Dynamic verb	**X** Jennifer <u>buys</u> a leather jacket.

We can use dynamic verbs in the present tense, but only if we use adverbs of frequency to make the action of the verb habitual or customary (and thus not time bound as dynamic verbs normally are):

Dynamic verb	Jennifer <u>buys</u> a leather jacket every time she goes to Italy.

We now return to the question of why it is so difficult for nonnative speakers to correct errors with stative verbs in the present progressive tense.

The answer probably lies in the unique way that the present progressive tense treats time. The very meaning of the tense name, "**progressive**," emphasizes that the whole purpose of the tense is to describe things that span (progress) across time. It would then seem that the span of time that is always implicit in the actions described in the present progressive tense would be perfectly compatible with the continuous nature of stative verbs. The fact that nonnative speakers so persistently use stative verbs in the present perfect tense shows that this idea makes sense to them.

However, this is not the case at all. The present progressive is always time limited and therefore totally incompatible with the timeless nature of stative verbs. To see why this is the case, let us look at some typical present progressive sentences (with dynamic verbs, naturally):

> Our team is really getting beat!
> We are completely revising our landscape plan.
> Did you hear that Janet Jones is running for mayor?

Note that none of these examples has any overt mention of an ending point or even of any expression of time. Instead, there is something much more subtle going on in these sentences. Whenever we use the present progressive tense, the action of the sentence exists in its own implied self-defined, self-limiting time frame. For example:

> Our team is really getting beat!

In this sentence, the action exists only as long as the game lasts.

> We are completely revising our landscape plan.

In this example, the action lasts however long it takes the speakers to revise their landscaping plan.

> Did you hear that Janet Jones is running for mayor?

In this third example, the action lasts however long Janet Jones's mayoral campaign lasts.

The most striking demonstration of the self-defined, self-limiting time frame of verbs in the present progressive is with verbs whose meaning would seem to make them inherently unlimited in terms of time. One such verb is *live*. Compare the meaning of the verb *live* in the present tense with the meaning of the same verb in the present progressive tense:

> *Present tense*   The Johnstons live in San Diego.
> (Meaning: The Johnstons permanently reside in San Diego.)

> *Present progressive*   The Johnstons are living in San Diego.
>   (Meaning: The Johnstons are staying in San Diego at the moment, but it is not
>   their permanent residence.)

Here is a second example with the verb *store*:

Present tense	We <u>store</u> all of our equipment in a warehouse.

(Meaning: We always keep our equipment in a warehouse.)

Present progressive	We <u>are storing</u> all of our equipment in a warehouse.

(Meaning: We are temporarily keeping our equipment in a warehouse.)

As you can see, when we change the tense of the verb from the present tense to the present progressive tense, the implicit time frame of the sentence also changes from unlimited to limited or temporary, that is, it becomes time bound.

As we have seen in this subsection on the use of the present progressive tense to express action in progress, the present progressive describes actions that span a period of time. Some nonnative speakers apparently think of this span of time as being equivalent to the "timeless" nature of tenses such as the present tense, which also describes action that spans across time. Accordingly, nonnative speakers assume that the present progressive tense, as with the present tense, is compatible with stative verbs. The difference is that the present progressive has a somewhat unusual self-limiting time frame that makes the present progressive time bound and therefore incompatible with the basic timeless meaning of stative verbs.

The key, then, for avoiding the highly persistent error of using stative verbs in the present progressive tense is twofold: (1) clearly understanding the odd way that the present progressive uses a self-limiting time frame, and (2) knowing how to reliably recognize stative verbs. This presentation suggested two specific features of stative verbs to be aware of: by far the most important is the different relationship between verb and subject. Stative verbs describe their subjects. Dynamic verbs carry out the actions that their subjects perform. The second feature of stative verbs is the incompatibility of stative verbs with most adverbs of time. Determining whether adverbs of time can be used with a verb is a helpful way of testing to see whether the verb is a timeless stative verb or a time-bound dynamic verb.

EXERCISE
10·3

*All of the following sentences are written in the present progressive tense. If the sentence is grammatical, write "OK." If the sentence is ungrammatical, mark the sentence with an "**X**" and replace the present progressive with an appropriate tense. The first two sentences are done as examples.*

The girls <u>are adoring</u> their new baby sister.

ANSWER: The girls **adore** their new baby sister.   **X**

The actors <u>are</u> still <u>stumbling</u> over their lines rather badly.

ANSWER: The actors <u>are</u> still <u>stumbling</u> over their lines rather badly.   OK

1. The baby <u>is being</u> hungry all the time.

2. Fortunately, we <u>are having</u> a laptop at our disposal.

3. I <u>am supervising</u> a new construction project.

4. The estimate <u>is including</u> all taxes and fees.

5. The kids <u>are mowing</u> the backyard this afternoon.

6. I <u>am hating</u> the fact that we are having so much trouble.

7. I don't think it <u>is harming</u> anyone.

8. The ceremony <u>is beginning</u> at 4 p.m.

9. They <u>are</u> all <u>liking</u> the company's new logo.

10. The heavy rain <u>is ruining</u> everyone's gardens.

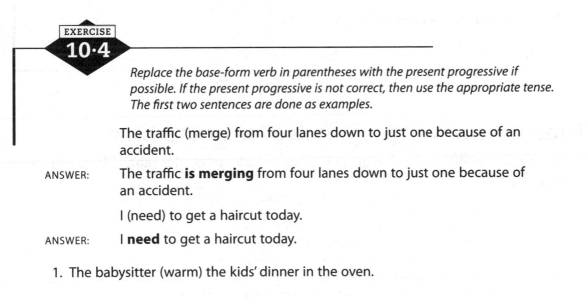

EXERCISE
10·4

Replace the base-form verb in parentheses with the present progressive if possible. If the present progressive is not correct, then use the appropriate tense. The first two sentences are done as examples.

The traffic (merge) from four lanes down to just one because of an accident.

ANSWER: The traffic **is merging** from four lanes down to just one because of an accident.

I (need) to get a haircut today.

ANSWER: I **need** to get a haircut today.

1. The babysitter (warm) the kids' dinner in the oven.

_____

2. The kids (want) to watch TV until bedtime.

_____

3. Their approval (mean) a lot to us.

_____

4. I told the waiter that we (celebrate) a birthday.

_____

5. George (know) where the restaurant is.

_____

6. The children (quarrel) again.

_____

7. We (soak) all of our dirty hiking clothes in the washing machine.

_____

8. The purse (belong) to that young lady over there.

_____

9. The tire (seem) a little flat to me.

_____

10. The flowers in the garden (bloom).

_____

Using the present progressive for future time

We often use the present progressive tense to talk about the future. Here are some examples:

> They are taking the night flight back.
> The flood is cresting within the next few days.
> We are visiting some old friends in Chicago next week.
> Ray and Joan are getting married next spring.
> The sun is setting tonight at 7:35.
> The government is announcing the new budget on Friday.
> Airline fares are going up next summer because of increasing fuel costs.
> Rio is hosting the summer Olympics in 2016.

Using the present progressive for the future is like using the present progressive for present time in one important respect: we cannot use the present progressive with stative verbs. For example, compare the use of the present progressive with the dynamic verb *start* and the stative verb *include*:

Dynamic verb	The meeting <u>is starting</u> at 2:30.
Stative verb	**X** The meeting <u>is including</u> an update on the budget.

We cannot use the stative verb *include* in the present progressive because, among other things, it is not time bound. The present progressive tense requires actions that take place in real time. The verb *include* is not really a time-bound action.

EXERCISE
10·5

All of the following sentences talk about future time using will, *which can be used equally well with both dynamic and stative verbs. Rewrite each sentence, replacing* will *with the corresponding present progressive verb form. If the resulting sentence is grammatical, label the sentence "OK" and write "Dynamic." If the resulting sentence is not grammatical, mark the sentence with an "X," draw a line through the present progressive verb, and write "Stative." The first two sentences are done as examples.*

The county <u>will hold</u> a special election on Tuesday.

ANSWER: OK   The county <u>is holding</u> a special election on Tuesday. **Dynamic**

We <u>will know</u> the results within 24 hours.

ANSWER: **X**   We ~~are knowing~~ the results within 24 hours. **Stative**

1. We <u>will hear</u> the results of the test soon.

_____

2. By Friday, you <u>will need</u> to give the animals food and fresh water.

_____

3. Getting an upgrade <u>will depend</u> on how much it costs.

_____

4. The company <u>will launch</u> its new product line in the fall.

_____

5. He <u>will undergo</u> surgery tomorrow morning.

_____

6. I <u>will buy</u> a ticket as soon as I know my dates.

_____

7. Mr. Green will retire at the end of the school year.

_____

8. My cousins will try to hike the entire north rim of the Grand Canyon this summer.

_____

9. They will recognize the hotel when they get there.

_____

10. They will certainly appreciate anything you can do for them.

In discussing the future tense in Chapter 4, we saw that we talk about the future in two main ways: (1) prediction and (2) intention. For example, compare the way the following two sentences use *will* to talk about the future:

Prediction	The reception will last until 10:00.
Intention	I will give you a call tomorrow.

The first sentence uses *will* to make a prediction about a future event. The second sentence uses *will* to express the speaker's intention to carry out an action in the future.

The same is true for using the present progressive to talk about the future. We can easily divide the earlier examples of the future-time use of the present progressive into two groups: (1) prediction and (2) intention:

Prediction
The flood is cresting within the next few days.
The sun is setting tonight at 7:35.
Airline fares are going up next summer because of increasing fuel costs.

Intention
They are taking the night flight back.
We are visiting some old friends in Chicago next week.
Ray and Joan are getting married next spring.
The government is announcing the new budget on Friday.
Rio is hosting the summer Olympics in 2016.

The key difference between prediction and intention is whether or not the subject of the sentence is the doer of the future action. In other words, if the subject is the agent that causes the future action to take place, we would classify the sentence as **intention.** However, another way to think about it is that all statements about the future are necessarily just predictions for the obvious reason that the future hasn't happened yet. However, there is an important subclass of future predictions in which the subjects are agents that intentionally cause (or at least try to cause) the future events to take place. This subclass, of course, is the group we classify as **intention**.

All of the following sentences use the present progressive tense to talk about the future. Classify each sentence as prediction or intention. The first two sentences are done as examples.

I am introducing the speaker at the 1:00 session.

ANSWER: Intention

A cold front from Canada is bringing record low temperatures for the weekend.

ANSWER: Prediction

1. The contractor is starting work on the renovation tomorrow.

   _____

2. The police are closing all the roads tonight because of the storm.

   _____

3. The last flight is departing tonight at 11:30.

   _____

4. The postgame interview is starting in a few minutes.

   _____

5. The president is addressing the country tonight at 6:00.

   _____

6. We are making an offer on their house this evening.

   _____

7. Jason and Mary are launching their boat for the first time when the tide comes in.

   _____

8. We <u>are switching</u> phone providers as soon as our existing contract is up.

_____

9. The court <u>is hearing</u> the case on March 27.

_____

10. The hurricane <u>is coming</u> ashore within the next few hours.

_____

The distinction between prediction and intention is important for using the present progressive because there are substantial differences in how we use the present progressive depending on whether we are talking about prediction or intention.

We will discuss the two uses of the present progressive in turn.

Using the present progressive for prediction

We typically use the present progressive for predictable events, that is, events that have been scheduled, have been planned, or are the outcome of some present action or arrangement; for example:

> The train <u>is leaving</u> from Grand Central Station.
> The game <u>is starting</u> at 12:30.
> The coach said that Norman <u>is playing</u> in the second half.

We cannot use the present progressive for mere personal or subjective guesses about the future. For example:

> **X** The market <u>is falling</u> 10 percent over the next three months.

This sentence is ungrammatical because the future behavior of the stock market cannot be scheduled, planned, or controlled by any present action or arrangement.

The description of when we use the present progressive to make predictions about future events is the same as the description of when we use the present tense to talk about the future. We have already said that we use the present tense to refer to future events if those events are fixed or scheduled.

The fact that the two tenses are virtually identical in their basic meanings would seem to imply that they are used interchangeably. Certainly in casual conversation they can be. However, the present progressive is typically used with an implication that the present tense lacks. To see the difference, compare the following two sentences:

Present tense	Delta flight 238 <u>departs</u> at 11:35.
Present progressive tense	Continental flight 332 <u>is departing</u> at 2:15.

The present tense is simply a factual statement about the Delta Airlines flight schedule. The use of the present progressive in the announcement about the Continental flight implies that information about the departure time is new or of special significance; very likely 2:15 is not the officially scheduled time but rather the newly rescheduled time for a delayed flight. When you are at an airport, public announcements of delays or gate changes are almost always given in the present progressive, calling attention to the fact that the information is new; for example:

> United flight 22 to Denver <u>is</u> now <u>departing</u> from gate 35.

Here are some more examples of this typical use of the present progressive for information that is new to the recipients of the information:

> The concerts <u>are starting</u> at 7:30 instead of 8:00 this year.
> The school bus <u>is coming</u> 15 minutes late this week.
> Because of the weather, the award presentation is <u>moving</u> to the gym.

We often use the present progressive to ask questions to confirm our understanding of scheduled, planned, or arranged events; for example:

> <u>Is</u> the game <u>starting</u> at 1:00?
> <u>Are</u> the children <u>going</u> to school tomorrow?
> <u>Is</u> Jayne <u>speaking</u> at the opening meeting?

Another use of the present progressive as opposed to the present tense is for emphasis. There is no necessary implication that the information is new to the recipient, but the use of the present progressive definitely brings the information to the attention of the recipient in an urgent way; for example:

> Hurry up, the game <u>is starting</u> in just a few minutes.
> Come on. The boat <u>is leaving</u> in 15 minutes.
> The taxi <u>is coming</u> in five minutes!

Using the present progressive for intention

We use the present progressive tense to make a factual statement about the subject's intention to carry out some future action. (Whether the speaker actually does carry out the future action is irrelevant.) Here are some examples:

> I <u>am working</u> from home tomorrow.
> The CEO <u>is announcing</u> the merger at the board meeting.
> We <u>are having</u> some friends over for lunch tomorrow. Can you join us?
> The painter <u>is finishing</u> the exterior this afternoon.

The present progressive is quite different from the other commonly used way of talking about the future: the helping verb *will*. *Will*, even when used with a human subject, is more likely to be a prediction or comment about the future rather than a statement of an intention to carry out a future action. For example, compare the different ways the two are used in the following pair of sentences:

Will	I'll see you tomorrow morning.
Present progressive	I am seeing you tomorrow morning.

The two sentences are completely different. *Will* is used to express a commonplace pleasantry about what will happen tomorrow. The sentence with the present progressive is not a conventional pleasantry; it is a personal commitment to carry out a specific action.

Will can be used to express commitment, but only if it is stressed; for example:

We will not let them get away with that!
I will do my very best.

However, if *will* is not stressed, there is typically no sense of emphasis or commitment. Unstressed *will*, even with a human subject, is often used for simple futurity; for example:

They will probably get in pretty late.
Nobody will want to go out tonight because we have an early flight tomorrow.
I'll see you later.

An important use of the present progressive for future time is asking yes-no questions about someone's present intention to carry out a future action. (Yes-no questions are questions that ask for only a "yes" or "no" answer.) Here are some examples:

Are you meeting anyone?
Is Cynthia calling a taxi?
Are the kids getting ready?
Is Larry thinking about going ahead anyway?

Be going to

The use of the present progressive for future time (for both prediction and intention) is greatly extended by the use of the present perfect helping verb construction *be going to* plus base-form verb. Here are two examples of this construction, the first using *be going to* for prediction and the second using it for intention:

Prediction	The weather is going to get colder next week.
Intention	The governor is going to veto the bill.

Adding the helping verb construction *be going to* does not noticeably change the meaning of present progressive. For example, compare the previous two example sentences with the same sentences used without the helping verb construction:

Present progressive plus be going to	The weather is going to get colder next week.
Present progressive tense	The weather is getting colder next week.
Present progressive plus be going to	The governor is going to veto the bill.
Present progressive tense	The governor is vetoing the bill.

There is no difference between the meanings of the two versions of the sentences. Nor is there any noticeable shift in emphasis or context between the two different versions. So, if adding *be going to* to present progressive sentences used for future time does not change meaning or emphasis, why bother doing it?

As we have already discussed, there is a general prohibition against using the present progressive tense with stative verbs. There is also a second, independent restriction against using the present progressive tense for predicting future events *unless* these events are scheduled, are planned, or are the outcome of some present action or arrangement.

When we use *be going to*, both of these restrictions are eliminated. That is, we can use *be going to* with stative verbs and we can use *be going to* for future events that are *not* scheduled, planned, or the outcome of some present action or arrangement.

Using *be going to* has the great advantage that we do not have to monitor the grammatically tricky present progressive for correctness.

Here are some examples of the first restriction: using stative verbs with the present progressive:

X The meeting tomorrow is including an update on the budget.
X They are agreeing to meet tomorrow.
X Higher prices are meaning lower sales later.

Here are the same stative verbs, but now with *be going to*:

The meeting tomorrow is going to include an update on the budget.
They are going to agree to meet tomorrow.
Higher prices are going to mean lower sales later.

As you can see, adding *be going to* makes the stative verbs completely grammatical in the present progressive.

All of the following sentences incorrectly use the present progressive tense with stative verbs. Correct these sentences by adding the helping verb construction be going to. *The first sentence is done as an example.*

X She <u>is loving</u> her new birthday present.

ANSWER: She <u>is going to love</u> her new birthday present.

1. **X** She <u>is being</u> on the executive committee starting next week.

   _____

2. **X** I <u>am having</u> some suggestions tomorrow.

   _____

3. **X** Their new apartment <u>is seeming</u> small after they move all their furniture in.

   _____

4. **X** He <u>is wanting</u> to get a new computer if he is going to work from home.

   _____

5. **X** Everyone <u>is knowing</u> soon enough.

   _____

6. **X** My parents <u>are needing</u> some help doing the paperwork.

   _____

7. **X** His actions <u>are seeming</u> pretty silly when the results come in.

   _____

8. **X** They <u>are promising</u> to behave in the future.

   _____

9. **X** His grades <u>are mattering</u> when he applies for a job.

   _____

10. **X** Their CEO <u>is agreeing</u> to be interviewed on the record.

   _____

The second restriction on the present progressive is that we cannot use the present progressive for predicting future events unless those events are scheduled, planned, or the result of some present action or arrangement.

Here are some examples of present progressive sentences that fail to meet these conditions and are ungrammatical as a result:

    X The weatherman said that it <u>is raining</u> tomorrow.
    X I believe that USC <u>is beating</u> UCLA next week.
    X The boys <u>are hurting</u> themselves unless they get better equipment.

When we add *be going to*, these same sentences all become fully grammatical:

    The weatherman said that it <u>is going to rain</u> tomorrow.
    I believe that USC <u>is going to beat</u> UCLA next week.
    The boys <u>are going to hurt</u> themselves unless they get better equipment.

EXERCISE
10·8

All of the following sentences incorrectly use the present progressive tense to predict future events because the events described cannot be scheduled, planned, or the result of some present action or arrangement. Correct these sentences by adding the helping verb construction be going to. *The first is done as an example.*

    X The favorite <u>is winning</u> this weekend's big horse race.

ANSWER: The favorite <u>is going to win</u> this weekend's big horse race.

1. **X** He <u>is earning</u> a lot of money when he graduates from college.

    _____

2. **X** I <u>am passing</u> tomorrow's test with flying colors.

    _____

3. **X** I think that the court <u>is ruling</u> in favor of our client.

    _____

4. **X** Many investors <u>are sitting</u> on the sidelines until after the new year.

    _____

5. **X** The Dow <u>is gaining</u> 10 percent by the end of the summer.

    _____

Idiomatic uses of the present progressive

There are two idiomatic uses of the present progressive: polite indirectness and comments on habitual behavior. These are mostly used in casual conversation rather than in formal writing.

Polite indirectness

English, as all other languages, has a number of ways of dealing with potentially awkward or embarrassing situations. One such technique is using the present progressive where we would normally expect the present tense in asking permission or expressing an opinion that might be offensive. Here are some examples, first in the present tense and then in the more polite present progressive tense:

Present	I <u>wonder</u> if I could take a minute of your time.
Present progressive	I <u>am wondering</u> if I could take a minute of your time.
Present	I <u>think</u> that you should reconsider your decision.
Present progressive	I <u>am thinking</u> that you should reconsider your decision.
Present	We <u>hope</u> to stay with you next week.
Present progressive	We <u>are hoping</u> to stay with you next week.

Comments on habitual behavior

We would normally talk about any kind of repeated or habitual action in the present tense; for example:

They <u>leave</u> their trash on our lawn.
He <u>interrupts</u> other people.
The mayor usually <u>puts</u> the blame for problems on somebody else.

There is an odd idiomatic use of the present progressive for commenting (quite negatively) on someone's habitual behavior. Compare the following pair of related sentences, the first in the present tense, the second in the present progressive:

Present	Carl always <u>comes</u> in to meetings late.
Present progressive	Carl <u>is</u> always <u>coming</u> in to meetings late.

These two sentences mean the same thing, but the sentence in the present progressive has a much more negative edge to it. The present tense sentence could be interpreted as a neutral statement of fact—that's just the way Carl is. The present progressive sentence, however, has two unmistakably negative implications: (1) Carl's coming in late is habitual, and (2) it is highly offensive (at least to this speaker).

The key to recognizing this meaning of the present progressive is the use of the adverb *always*. Here are some more examples:

> They <u>are</u> always <u>leaving</u> their trash on our lawn.
> He <u>is</u> always <u>interrupting</u> other people.
> The mayor <u>is</u> always <u>putting</u> the blame for problems on somebody else.
> Those birds <u>are</u> always <u>leaving</u> a mess on our deck.
> The tenor <u>is</u> always <u>coming</u> in half a beat late.

EXERCISE
10·9

All of the following sentences use the present progressive correctly. Identify which of the four meanings of the present progressive each sentence uses: (1) action in progress, (2) future, (3) polite indirectness, or (4) habitual behavior. The first is done as an example.

They <u>are meeting</u> with the contractor as soon as they can.

ANSWER: (2) future

1. I'm <u>getting</u> a busy signal.

_____

2. We <u>are driving</u> my mother to see the doctor in Chicago later.

_____

3. He's always <u>taking</u> the easy way out.

_____

4. I'm <u>hoping</u> that I can get in to see you this afternoon.

_____

5. The schoolkids <u>are</u> always <u>crossing</u> the street against the light.

_____

6. The builders <u>are putting</u> in the new flooring on Wednesday.

_____

7. Everyone <u>is talking</u> about how much gas costs.

_____

8. I'm <u>getting</u> a lot of static on the phone. I'll call you right back.

_____

9. They <u>are going</u> out to dinner tonight.

_____

10. We <u>are asking</u> for a few minutes of your time to bring you an important message.

_____

The past progressive tense

The past progressive tense consists of the helping verb *be* in a past tense form followed by a verb in the present participle *-ing* form. Here are some examples:

> We were <u>driving</u> downtown when the storm hit.
> The train <u>was</u> just <u>pulling</u> into the station when we got there.
> We <u>were thinking</u> about going out for dinner.
> I <u>was thinking</u> I might go camping this weekend.
> I <u>was talking</u> to Janet yesterday, and she told me that you were retiring.
> We <u>were working</u> on that project all morning!

Major use of the past progressive tense

The major function of the past progressive tense is very much like the basic function of the present progressive tense: to talk about something that takes place (i.e., "progresses") over some span of time—present time for the present progressive, past time for the past progressive. There are also a number of other, more idiomatic uses of the past progressive that we will discuss at the end of the chapter.

Another important point of similarity between the two tenses is that the past progressive (as with the present progressive) can be used only with **dynamic** verbs. (Chapter 10 has a detailed explanation of why.) Dynamic verbs are verbs whose action takes place in real time (as opposed to the inherently timeless nature of **stative** verbs). Consequently, dynamic verbs are compatible with the time-bound meaning of the past progressive tense. For example, notice that all of the examples of the past progressive given at the beginning of this chapter are dynamic verbs.

By the same token, the timeless nature of stative verbs makes them incompatible with the time-bound meaning of the past perfect tense. (Please see Chapter 1 if you need to review the characteristics of dynamic and stative verbs.) For example, the verb *like* is a typical stative verb that describes an ongoing state or condition. We cannot use this stative verb in the past progressive tense:

X I <u>was</u> always <u>liking</u> homemade ice cream.

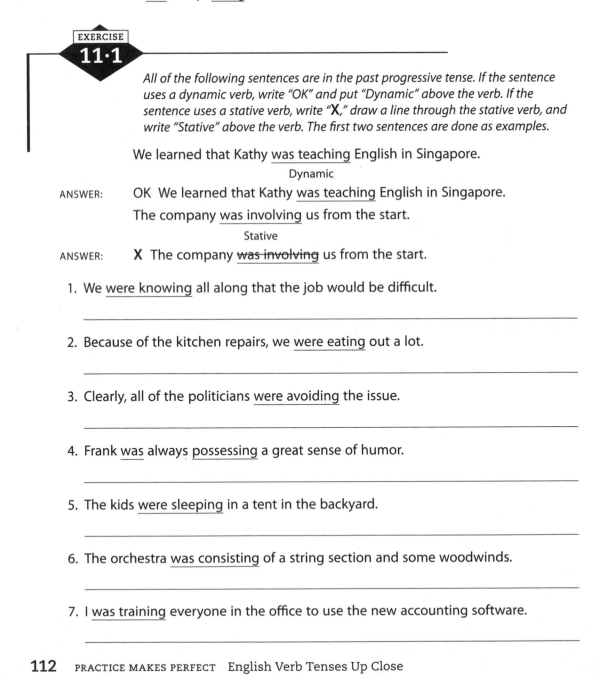

EXERCISE
11·1

All of the following sentences are in the past progressive tense. If the sentence uses a dynamic verb, write "OK" and put "Dynamic" above the verb. If the sentence uses a stative verb, write "X," draw a line through the stative verb, and write "Stative" above the verb. The first two sentences are done as examples.

We learned that Kathy <u>was teaching</u> English in Singapore.

Dynamic

ANSWER: OK We learned that Kathy <u>was teaching</u> English in Singapore.

The company <u>was involving</u> us from the start.

Stative

ANSWER: **X** The company <u>was involving</u> us from the start.

1. We <u>were knowing</u> all along that the job would be difficult.

   _____

2. Because of the kitchen repairs, we <u>were eating</u> out a lot.

   _____

3. Clearly, all of the politicians <u>were avoiding</u> the issue.

   _____

4. Frank <u>was</u> always <u>possessing</u> a great sense of humor.

   _____

5. The kids <u>were sleeping</u> in a tent in the backyard.

   _____

6. The orchestra <u>was consisting</u> of a string section and some woodwinds.

   _____

7. I <u>was training</u> everyone in the office to use the new accounting software.

   _____

8. The government <u>was encouraging</u> everyone to get flu shots.

   _____

9. After it started raining, the kids <u>were wanting</u> to go home.

   _____

10. Everyone <u>was needing</u> to take a break because of the heat.

   _____

Both the past tense and the past progressive describe actions that took place in past time. The difference between the two is that the past tense treats the past-time action as a finished event—completely over and done with—whereas the past progressive treats the past-time action as an ongoing process that continues through some span of past time. For example, compare the following sentences:

Past tense	Fred <u>mowed</u> the lawn this afternoon. (event)
Past progressive	Fred <u>was mowing</u> the lawn this afternoon. (process)

The past tense sentence describes an action that was completed in the past. The past progressive sentence describes an action that was in process during the time frame of the sentence. We have no way of knowing whether or not Fred ever finished mowing the lawn. The past progressive sentence is not about what happened as a completed event; the sentence is about what was going on at or during some particular moment or period of past time.

EXERCISE
11·2

Each of the following sentences contains an underlined verb in its base form. Put the verb into its proper past tense or past progressive form according to whether the sentence describes an event (past tense) or a process (past progressive tense). The first two sentences are done as examples.

Some people <u>talk</u> all during the movie. (process)

ANSWER: Some people <u>were talking</u> all during the movie.

We <u>collect</u> the samples only in the early morning. (event)

ANSWER: We <u>collected</u> the samples only in the early morning.

1. The cold weather threaten to ruin the entire crop. (event)

   _____

2. The country slowly emerge from financial chaos. (process)

   _____

3. During the whole time, I try to get a word in edgewise. (process)

   _____

4. The company rapidly expand into Asian markets. (event)

   _____

5. As it turned out, the police record the entire conversation. (process)

   _____

6. The heavy truck traffic damage the road surfaces. (process)

   _____

7. The company represent some of the firms in the industry. (event)

   _____

8. All the noise frighten the children. (process)

   _____

9. The kids swim at the pool in the community center. (process)

   _____

10. Their lawyer advise them not to say anything about what happened. (event)

   _____

As we have seen, the past progressive functions much as does the present progressive in that they both describe actions in progress. There is, however, one way in which the two types of progressive tenses are not the same, especially when they use verbs with a strong sentence of action.

Compare the following examples of present progressive and past progressive sentences. Assume that there is no previous mention of these sentences, that is, you are seeing each sentence for the first time:

Present progressive	My parents are traveling in India.
Past progressive	My parents were traveling in India.

The present progressive sentence seems perfectly normal. However, the past progressive sentence as it stands seems unfinished or inconclusive in a way the present progressive sentence does not.

The difference is in the time of the action. Sentences in the present progressive tense take place in a time that is automatically defined: now—at the present moment of time. We always know when sentences in the present progressive tense take place: they take place *now*.

Sentences in the past progressive, however, are different. There is nothing that automatically defines when they took place in the past *unless* the producers of the sentences provide that information for us. That is why the example sentence about traveling in India seems incomplete in the past progressive. We have no way to place the trip to India in past time.

To make the sentence seem complete, we need to add what is called a "temporal frame." A temporal frame is an adverbial time expression that locates the action of the sentence in past time—either by providing a point in time or a span of time during which the action took place. Here are some examples of the same sentence with the temporal frame added (in italics):

> My parents <u>were traveling</u> in India *recently.*
> My parents <u>were traveling</u> in India *during my junior year.*
> My parents <u>were traveling</u> in India *when the attack in Mumbai happened.*

The sentences with the temporal frame added now seem complete and perfectly normal. Note that the three examples of temporal frames use all three different types of adverbials:

> *Recently* is an adverb.
> *During my junior year* is an adverb prepositional phrase.
> *When the attack in Mumbai happened* is an adverb clause.

All temporal frames are adverbials of time—adverbs, adverb prepositional phrases, or adverb clauses. Adverbials of time (as with most other adverbials) typically follow the verb in what is called **normal order**. One of the defining characteristics of adverbials of time (again, as with most adverbials) is that they can be moved to the beginning of the sentence in what is called **inverted order**. Here are the three example sentences again, both in normal order and in inverted order:

Adverb

Normal order	My parents <u>were traveling</u> in India *recently.*
Inverted order	*Recently* my parents <u>were traveling</u> in India.

Adverb prepositional phrase

Normal order	My parents <u>were traveling</u> in India *during my junior year.*
Inverted order	*During my junior year*, my parents <u>were traveling</u> in India.

Adverb clause

Normal order	My parents <u>were traveling</u> in India *when the attack in Mumbai happened.*
Inverted order	*When the attack in Mumbai happened,* my parents <u>were traveling</u> in India.

Note that when an adverb clause is inverted, that is, the adverb clause is moved from its normal place following the main clause to a position in front of the main clause, the inverted adverb clause is set off with a comma. Unlike in British English where the use of commas with inverted adverb clauses is optional, in American English the commas are obligatory.

**EXERCISE
11·3**

Each of the following sentences is in the past progressive tense. Each sentence contains an adverbial of time that functions as a temporal frame for that sentence. Underline the entire temporal frame. Confirm that your answer is correct by moving the entire temporal frame adverbial to the beginning of the sentence. (Remember, if you invert an adverb clause, be sure to use a comma.) The first sentence is done as an example.

A film crew was shooting a commercial in front of our building all morning.

ANSWER: A film crew was shooting a commercial in front of our building <u>all morning</u>.

CONFIRMATION: <u>All morning</u>, a film crew was shooting a commercial in front of our building.

1. I was listening to the radio on the way to work.

   _____

   Confirmation: _____

2. Everybody was completely on edge after what happened.

   _____

   Confirmation: _____

3. The water was flooding the lower fields after all the heavy rains.

   _____

   Confirmation: _____

4. They were performing at schools around the state during the fall.

_____

Confirmation: _____

5. The police were still questioning witnesses even after the trial started.

_____

Confirmation: _____

6. The wind was blowing faster than 100 miles an hour during the worst of the storm.

_____

Confirmation: _____

7. The manager was interviewing ski instructors over the Thanksgiving break.

_____

Confirmation: _____

8. She was working on her master's degree then.

_____

Confirmation: _____

9. I was just quitting for the night when the alarm sounded.

_____

Confirmation: _____

10. Things were looking pretty bad for our candidate before we got the new poll results.

_____

Confirmation: _____

Sentences with adverb clauses can be quite confusing. One thing that makes them confusing, as we have seen, is that the main clause and the adverb clause can be in either order; for example:

> The teams <u>were</u> already <u>playing</u> *by the time we got to the stadium.*
> main clause   adverb clause

> *By the time we got to the stadium*, the teams <u>were</u> already <u>playing</u>.
> adverb clause   main clause

There is a second reason why sentences with adverb clauses can be confusing. So far, all of our examples with adverb clauses have had the past perfect verb tense in the main clause and the temporal frame in the adverb clause. However, there is no grammatical requirement that the past perfect verb tense be in the main clause. It can be (and often is) in the adverb clause; for example:

I got interested in Asian art *when I was living in San Francisco*.
main clause   adverb clause

And, of course, to add to the confusion, the adverb clause with the past progressive tense can also be inverted; for example:

When I was living in San Francisco, I got interested in Asian art.
adverb clause   main clause

EXERCISE
11·4

This is a different type of exercise that mimics the options we have when we actually form real sentences. Each of the following sentences consists of two clauses, the first labeled "main clause" and the second labeled "adverb clause." Follow these steps to create two versions of the same sentence:
    Step 1: Identify and underline the two verbs that make up the past progressive tense (hint: they can be in either clause).
    Step 2: Attach the adverb clause to the end of the main clause to create a complete sentence with the adverb clause in the normal position following the main clause.
    Step 3: Form an inverted version of the same sentence by attaching the adverb clause to the beginning of the sentence (hint: check the punctuation).
    The first sentence is done as an example.

Main clause: I was just getting into the shower

Adverb clause: When the phone rang

ANSWER: Step 1: I <u>was</u> just <u>getting</u> into the shower

Step 2: I <u>was</u> just <u>getting</u> into the shower when the phone rang.

Step 3: When the phone rang, I <u>was</u> just <u>getting</u> into the shower.

1. Main clause: I was reading a book on my Kindle

Adverb clause: While everyone else relaxed by the pool

Step 1: _____

Step 2: _____

Step 3: _____

2. Main clause: My father suffered a minor stroke

   Adverb clause: When he was undergoing surgery

   Step 1: _____

   Step 2: _____

   Step 3: _____

3. Main clause: The troops were storing ammunition

   Adverb clause: When the big explosion happened

   Step 1: _____

   Step 2: _____

   Step 3: _____

4. Main clause: They were shutting the door

   Adverb clause: After the horse was stolen

   Step 1: _____

   Step 2: _____

   Step 3: _____

5. Main clause: The campers were packing up all their gear

   Adverb clause: When the storm finally broke

   Step 1: _____

   Step 2: _____

   Step 3: _____

6. Main clause: I got all the dishes done

   Adverb clause: While you were talking on the phone

   Step 1: _____

   Step 2: _____

   Step 3: _____

7. Main clause: The fund was investing in Swiss francs

   Adverb clause: Whenever the dollar was overvalued

   Step 1: _____

   Step 2: _____

   Step 3: _____

8. Main clause: We would make the kids give us their cell phones

   Adverb clause: Every time they were doing their homework

   Step 1: _____

   Step 2: _____

   Step 3: _____

9. Main clause: The birds were building nests

   Adverb clause: Whenever they could find a protected place

   Step 1: _____

   Step 2: _____

   Step 3: _____

10. Main clause: Our flights were always late

   Adverb clause: When we were flying in or out of Newark

   Step 1: _____

   Step 2: _____

   Step 3: _____

Idiomatic uses of the past progressive tense

There are six idiomatic uses of the past progressive. All of these idiomatic uses are much more likely to be used in casual conversation than in formal writing, and, of course, it is for just that reason that even advanced nonnative speakers are unlikely to be aware that these idiomatic uses even exist. In casual conversation, these idiomatic uses are fairly common and often convey significant information, attitudes, and social commentaries.

Here, roughly in order of frequency, are the six idiomatic uses. Each of the six will be discussed in detail with examples.

- ◆ Polite questions and requests
- ◆ Tentative suggestions
- ◆ Habitual actions
- ◆ Failed plans or actions
- ◆ Reported informal conversation
- ◆ Disclaiming previous plans or information

Polite questions and requests

> I was wondering if you could help me.
> We were hoping that you could join us.
> Was your son finished playing with that toy?

We have seen in previous chapters that both the past tense and the progressive tense are associated with polite indirectness. It is thus no surprise that a tense that is both past and progressive is used as a polite form for questions and requests. Note that when we make requests of strangers or people that we want to show deference to, we often frame a request as a question; for example:

> Were you using those chairs?

really means

> We want to use those chairs; is that OK with you?

Tentative suggestions

> I was thinking we might go camping this weekend.
> I was wondering if it might make sense to make them an offer.
> I am suggesting that we talk it over before we make a decision we will regret.

The use of the past progressive to make a suggestion signals that the person or persons making the suggestion is doing so in a tentative way that recognizes that others may have valid reasons for not agreeing with it.

Habitual actions

One meaning of the past progressive is to describe actions that were habitual at some point or period in the past. Here are some examples:

> The kids <u>were playing</u> football at every recess.
> I <u>was listening</u> to classical jazz all the time.
> The brakes <u>were</u> constantly <u>pulling</u> to the right.

There is no implication that the action that was habitual in the past continues on to the present time or will continue into the future. Instead, there is a strong implication that the habitual action is strictly limited to the past or to the past situation in which the behavior occurred.

There is an important variation in the habitual use of the past progressive in informal conversation that requires the use of the adverb *always*. Here are some examples:

> Jackson <u>was</u> always <u>falling</u> asleep in class.
> The trumpet player <u>was</u> always <u>coming</u> in a little late.
> When we lived there, people <u>were</u> always <u>blocking</u> the driveway.

Notice that all three of these sentences give examples of negative behavior. This is typical for this use of the past progressive with *always*, which signals that the speaker is quite critical of the behavior being described. The use of the past progressive with *always* implies that the behavior was deliberate and persistent rather than being the result of an accidental moment of thoughtlessness, and this implication can have a sharp edge to it.

Failed plans or actions

> We **were** going camping this weekend, but we won't be in this weather.
> I **was** planning on going home early, but it doesn't look as though I can now.
> Well, we **were** flying out tomorrow morning, but . . .

The key to recognizing this use of the past progressive is the unusually heavy stress on *was* or *were*. The meaning of this use of the past progressive is something along the lines of, "Well, this is what I/we planned to do, but it probably is not going to happen." Often, speakers will not actually finish the sentence beyond the *but* (as in the third example). Instead, they will let their voices trail off into silence with a dropping intonation so that the vowel in *but* is drawn out.

Reported informal conversation

I was talking to Bob yesterday, and he mentioned that you were retiring.
We were talking to the director, and she said the contract might not be renewed.
I was talking to him in the elevator, and he said you were changing offices.

This is a rather subtle use of the past progressive. It is a way of issuing a kind of disclaimer about how the information was obtained. It implies that the information was the result of a casual, informal, almost accidental conversation and that the source of the information was not speaking formally or on the record. It also implies that the person using the past progressive did not deliberately seek out this information.

To see the difference between normal reporting of conversation in the past tense and this use of the past progressing, compare the following conversations. Assume that John is the person doing the speaking in both sentences.

Normal reporting in past tense	Fred told me that your CEO might quit.
Past progressive tense	I was talking to Fred, and he told me that your CEO might quit.

The first sentence is essentially public information. The speaker (John) is willing to be quoted as the source of information. The second sentence is much more indirect. The speaker (John) is passing on information that he heard from Fred, but by using the past progressive tense, John is signaling that what he heard from Fred was from spontaneous, casual conversation not really meant to be taken as public information.

Disclaiming previous plans or information

Everyone was getting together after work, I think.
We were eating in the hotel as far as I know.
Terry was making her presentation at 4:00.

This is another subtle use of the past progressive for the purpose of making a disclaimer. In this case, the speaker is making a disclaimer about the accuracy of the information the speaker is about to provide. Here is an example of a situation in which this construction might be used. Suppose that someone asked you this question:

"When is Mary's flight landing?"

If you knew for a fact that it was due at 8:30 and had no reason to think it would not land then, you would probably answer in either the present tense or the present progressive (echoing the tense used in the question):

"It lands at 8:30."
"It is landing at 8:30."

Now suppose that your information was not very current or that you had some doubt about its accuracy. In that case, you would signal your uncertainty by answering in the past progressive tense:

"It <u>was landing</u> at 8:30 last I heard."

Look again at the three examples at the beginning of this discussion. All of them have this implication: "Well, this was the plan, but I don't really know if it is actually going to happen or not."

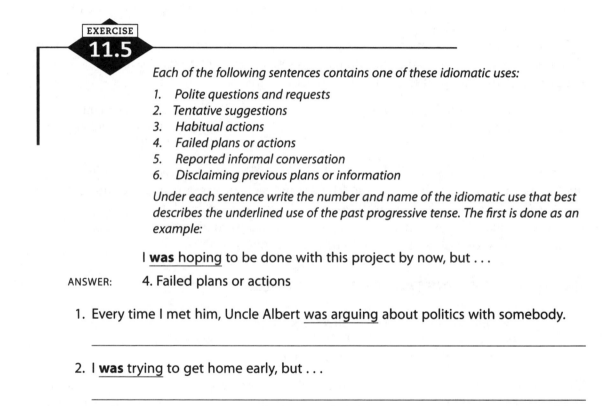

11.5

Each of the following sentences contains one of these idiomatic uses:

1. *Polite questions and requests*
2. *Tentative suggestions*
3. *Habitual actions*
4. *Failed plans or actions*
5. *Reported informal conversation*
6. *Disclaiming previous plans or information*

Under each sentence write the number and name of the idiomatic use that best describes the underlined use of the past progressive tense. The first is done as an example:

I **was** <u>hoping</u> to be done with this project by now, but . . .

ANSWER: 4. Failed plans or actions

1. Every time I met him, Uncle Albert <u>was arguing</u> about politics with somebody.

   _____

2. I **was** <u>trying</u> to get home early, but . . .

   _____

3. We <u>were wondering</u> if you would like to share a cab.

   _____

4. Well, we **were** <u>hoping</u> to sell the house, but not with the real estate market the way it is now.

   _____

5. The consultants <u>were meeting</u> with us at 5:00 last I heard.

   _____

6. I <u>was thinking</u> that we should invite the neighbors over for dinner sometime.

_____

7. <u>Were</u> you still <u>using</u> the salad dressing?

_____

8. The sprinkler system <u>was</u> always <u>going</u> off at the wrong times.

_____

9. I <u>was talking</u> to Mr. Green recently, and he said you might be moving.

_____

10. I <u>was suggesting</u> that we might reduce our asking price.

_____

The future progressive tense

The future progressive tense consists of the helping verb *be* in its future tense form *will be* followed by a verb in the present participle *–ing* form. Here are some examples:

> We will be staying with some friends in Los Angeles.
> I will be waiting for you in the baggage claim area.
> The painters will be finishing up the kitchen tomorrow.
> The storm will be hitting the coast around midnight.
> Everyone will be watching the big game.
> I'll be loading the car while you check out of the motel.

Major use of the future progressive tense

The basic meaning of the future progressive tense is to talk about something that is expected to take place (i.e., "progresses") over some span of future time. There are also four other, more idiomatic uses of the future progressive tense that we will discuss at the end of the chapter.

The future progressive tense, as with the other two progressive tenses, can generally be used only with **dynamic** verbs and not with **stative** verbs.

Strangely enough, there is a special and quite limited use of the future progressive tense that does permit it to be used with some stative verbs. We will ignore this highly restricted use of the future progressive until we get to the discussion of idiomatic uses at the end of the chapter.

Here are some examples of the future progressive using both types of verbs:

> **Dynamic verbs**
> The fish will be biting after all this rain.
> I'll be working downstairs if you need me.
> It will be snowing all afternoon.

Stative verbs

X You <u>will be loving</u> your new kitchen when it is finished.

X They <u>will be agreeing</u> with you.

X I am afraid that it <u>will be costing</u> more than we can afford.

EXERCISE 12·1

All of the following sentences are in the future progressive tense. If the sentence uses a dynamic verb, write "OK" and put "Dynamic" above the verb. If the sentence uses a stative verb, write "X," draw a line through the stative verb, and write "Stative" above the verb. The first two sentences are done as examples.

They <u>will be discussing</u> the agreement for hours yet.

Dynamic

ANSWER: OK They <u>will be discussing</u> the agreement for hours yet.

He <u>will be belonging</u> to a fraternity when he is in college.

Stative

ANSWER: **X** He ~~will be belonging~~ to a fraternity when he is in college.

1. I <u>will be seeing</u> about it and let you know what I find out.

2. The electrician <u>will be rewiring</u> the kitchen on Monday.

3. Their children <u>will be looking</u> just like them.

4. They <u>will not be minding</u> it if we park in their driveway.

5. The committee <u>will be counting</u> votes tomorrow.

6. The team <u>will be deserving</u> its reputation if they can win today.

7. The kids <u>will be playing</u> on the swings all afternoon.

8. The dinner <u>will not be including</u> dessert or beverage.

9. The company <u>will be expanding</u> its online information system.

10. Ruth <u>will be playing</u> tennis this afternoon with some of her friends.

The future progressive is like the past progressive in one important way: the need to define when the action takes place by adding what is called a "temporal frame" to the sentence. (See Chapter 11 for a detailed discussion of temporal frames.) For example:

My parents <u>will be visiting</u> us.

This sentence seems incomplete without giving more information about the visit, either when the visit will take place (time) or how long the visit will be (duration). When we revise the sentence by adding a temporal frame (in italics), the sentence seems complete:

My parents <u>will be visiting</u> us *after Christmas.* (time)
My parents <u>will be visiting</u> us *for a couple of days.* (duration)

Temporal frames are always adverbials of time or duration; they can be adverbs, adverb prepositional phrases, or adverb clauses. Here is an example of each type in italics:

We <u>will be backpacking</u> in the Sierras *next week.* (adverb)
We <u>will be backpacking</u> in the Sierras *during spring break.* (adverb prepositional phrase)
We <u>will be backpacking</u> in the Sierras *while we are on vacation.* (adverb clause)

All of these adverbials of time and duration share the characteristic that they can be moved from their normal position at the end of the sentence to an **inverted** position at the beginning of the sentence; for example:

Next week, we <u>will be backpacking</u> in the Sierras.
During spring break, we <u>will be backpacking</u> in the Sierras.
While we are on vacation, we <u>will be backpacking</u> in the Sierras.

Note that the inverted adverb clause is followed by a comma. The use of commas with inverted adverb clauses is obligatory in American English.

EXERCISE
12·2

Each of the following sentences is in the future progressive tense and contains an adverbial of time that functions as a temporal frame for that sentence. Underline the entire temporal frame. Confirm that your answer is correct by moving the entire temporal frame adverbial to the beginning of the sentence. (Remember, if you invert an adverb clause, be sure to use a comma.) The first sentence is done as an example.

The band will be playing in Denver next Friday and Saturday.

ANSWER: The band will be playing in Denver <u>next Friday and Saturday.</u>

CONFIRMATION: <u>Next Friday and Saturday,</u> the band will be playing in Denver.

1. The principal will be judging the spelling competition at 1 p.m.

_____

2. They will be living in Spain until the end of the summer.

_____

3. We will be continuing the discussion after everyone finishes dinner.

_____

4. We will be closing down the beach house after Labor Day.

_____

5. The sales staff will be showing the apartment as soon as it is vacant.

_____

6. Department heads will be meeting with the CFO every Monday morning.

_____

7. They will be expecting us to begin discussions the minute we get off the plane.

_____

8. I will be teaching Accounting 101 in the winter quarter.

_____

9. They will be getting married after she graduates.

_____

10. Maintenance will be replacing all the old carpets over the holidays.

_____

Both the future tense and the future progressive are used to describe an action that will take place in future time, but the two tenses look at the future action in two very different ways: the future tense describes the action as a unitary **event** that happens at a single point in future time. The future progressive tense, however, is used to emphasize that the future action is a **process** that occurs across a span or period of future time; for example:

Future tense	We <u>will host</u> a reception for the sales force tomorrow.
Future progressive tense	We <u>will be hosting</u> a reception for the sales force tomorrow.

Even if the two sentences are talking about the same reception, the two tenses look at it in two different ways: the future tense sentence sees the reception as a single event (as opposed to all other possible events or not doing an event at all); the future progressive tense sees the reception as a process or sustained action that takes place across a period of time.

Each of the following sentences contains an underlined verb in its base form. Put the verb into its proper future tense or future progressive form according to whether the sentence describes an event (future tense) or a process (future progressive). The first two sentences are done as examples.

The marketing department <u>fund</u> tomorrow's reception. (event)

ANSWER: The marketing department <u>will fund</u> tomorrow's reception.

The light <u>fade</u> by the time we get to the campground. (process)

ANSWER: The light <u>will be fading</u> by the time we get to the campground.

1. Everyone <u>rush</u> to get their taxes in before the April 15 deadline. (process)

   _____

2. This last payment <u>fulfill</u> the terms of the contract. (event)

   _____

3. Everyone <u>check</u> their roofs for damage as soon as this terrible wind lets up. (process)

   _____

4. The governor <u>announce</u> the winners of the state awards at the banquet. (event)

   _____

5. On the first day of school all the kids <u>cling</u> to their parents. (process)

   _____

6. Henry <u>edit</u> the white paper before we send it out for review. (process)

   _____

7. Everyone <u>notice</u> that Pat is gone. (event)

   _____

8. They <u>fish</u> until it gets too dark to bait their hooks. (process)

   _____

9. I <u>grab</u> a bite at the cafeteria before I go to the meeting. (event)

_____

10. All the rivers <u>overflow</u> their banks after all this rain. (process)

_____

Idiomatic uses of the future progressive tense

There are four idiomatic uses of the future progressive. As is typically the case with idiomatic uses, they are most common in casual conversation. Here, in order of frequency, are the four uses:

◆ Planned or expected future event
◆ Imagining how someone else feels or thinks
◆ Indirect invitation or request
◆ Ironic imaginary future

Planned or expected future event

This is a fairly common use of the future progressive, even though it is constrained to certain circumstances. We use it to talk about a future event or action that is already arranged or planned. This use is sometimes described as "the future as a matter of course." It is often used for announcements, especially announcements aboard airplanes; for example:

> We <u>will be closing</u> the cabin door shortly.
> We <u>will be serving</u> a light breakfast before we land.
> We <u>will be cruising</u> at an altitude of 35,000 feet.
> We <u>will be landing</u> in approximately 20 minutes.

In terms of basic meaning, these announcements could have been given in the future tense just as well as in the future progressive, but there is a reason why airline companies prefer the future progressive: the use of the future progressive implies that the future action is in accordance with an established plan. In other words, everything is according to schedule and under control. Compare the following examples:

Future tense	We <u>will land</u> in approximately 20 minutes.
Future progressive tense	We <u>will be landing</u> in approximately 20 minutes.

The information in the future tense sentence could be new or unexpected information. However, the information in the future progressive sentence is comfortably routine.

Here are some more examples of the future progressive that do not involve airplanes:

> I'll be seeing Alice this weekend, and I will ask her then.

In this sentence, the speaker's use of the future progressive lets the listener know that the speaker's meeting with Alice has already been arranged, so it is no inconvenience for the speaker to meet with Alice.

> You can recognize Ronald because he will be driving a blue Volvo convertible.

The speaker's use of the future progressive lets the listener know that he or she can count on Ronald's driving a blue Volvo convertible.

> When you get to your hotel, a representative from the travel agency will be waiting for you with your tickets.

The speaker's use of the future progressive reassures the listener that the plans will be carried out in a completely predictable and orderly manner.

Imagining how someone else feels or thinks

In this use, the future progressive signals that the speaker is making a hypothetical statement about what someone else might be feeling or thinking. Here are some examples:

> They will be wondering what happened to us.
> John will be thinking that we have got lost.
> They will be wishing they had stayed at home.
> They will be worrying about the icy roads.
> He will be wishing he had brought cooler clothing.

Indirect invitation or request

> You will be getting hungry, I suspect.
> You will be wanting to get those wet shoes off.
> You will be wanting to wash up before dinner.
> You will be needing some extra time.

This use of the future progressive is like the previous one in that it imagines how someone else feels, but it functions quite differently. Depending on the context, this use can be either a polite question or an indirect request. In either case, it requires the person being addressed to make a yes or no response.

Ironic imaginary future

In this use of the future progressive tense, the speaker deliberately exaggerates someone's actions or behavior to a ridiculous extreme to call attention to how remarkable that person's actual actions or behavior really were. For example, if a child who has always refused to eat any kind of vegetable one day eats a few peas without the usual fuss, a parent might make this remark:

Next, he <u>will be liking</u> spinach and broccoli.

This is a way of pointing out how special it was for the child to eat the peas. (The joke here is based on the fact that even children who like most vegetables don't usually like strong-tasting vegetables such as spinach and broccoli.)

The key to recognizing this odd use of the future progressive is the word *next*, which implies an imaginary series or sequence of events: if a person does action A (eating a few peas in our example), doing A will logically lead to doing action B (eating spinach and broccoli). Because we all know that action B is remarkable or preposterous or absurd, we can see that the person's original action A is equally remarkable or preposterous or absurd.

Here is another example. Suppose that in a trial about an automobile accident, a lawyer believes that the opposing lawyer, Mr. Smith, is denying something that is true. The lawyer might say this:

Next, Mr. Smith <u>will be denying</u> that the accident even happened.

This is a way of pointing out how absurd Mr. Smith's original denial is.

Here are some more examples of this use of the future progressive.

She <u>will be owning</u> her own business, next.
He <u>will be believing</u> in the Easter Bunny, next.
Next, he <u>will be wanting</u> his own car.

One of the many odd things about this construction is that it is often used with stative verbs, which are normally totally ungrammatical when used in any progressive tenses. All of the verbs used in the five examples of this construction are stative verbs: *like, deny, own, believe,* and *want.*

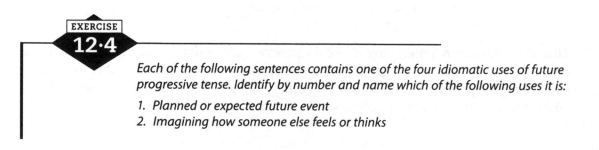

EXERCISE

12·4

Each of the following sentences contains one of the four idiomatic uses of future progressive tense. Identify by number and name which of the following uses it is:

1. Planned or expected future event
2. Imagining how someone else feels or thinks

3. *Indirect invitation or request*
4. *Ironic imaginary future*

The first sentence is done as an example.

All of the men <u>will be wearing</u> coats and ties.

ANSWER: 1. Planned or expected future event

1. We <u>will</u> all <u>be wishing</u> we had gotten to bed earlier.

_____

2. Next, you <u>will be running</u> a marathon.

_____

3. They <u>will be wondering</u> where everybody went.

_____

4. You <u>will be wanting</u> to get to bed soon.

_____

5. We <u>will be serving</u> dinner at 8:00.

_____

6. Everybody <u>will be needing</u> to take a break soon.

_____

7. The nonstop train for Chicago <u>will be arriving</u> on track 12.

_____

8. You <u>will be wanting</u> some hot coffee, I imagine.

_____

9. This year we <u>will be observing</u> the holiday on Monday.

_____

10. They <u>will be wanting</u> to have their own tennis court, next.

_____

The perfect progressive tenses

The perfect progressive tenses are a combination of one of the three perfect tenses (past perfect, present perfect, future perfect) with the progressive tense.

The perfect tenses consist of the helping verb *have* (in some form: present, past, or future) followed by a verb in the past participle form. In the following examples, the verb *fade* is in the past participle form.

Present perfect	The carpet **has** faded near the windows.
Past perfect	The carpet **had** faded near the windows.
Future perfect	The carpet **will have** faded near the windows.

The progressive tense consists of the helping verb *be* in some form followed by a verb in the present participle form; for example:

They <u>are celebrating</u> his birthday today.

When we combine the perfect and the progressive tenses, the perfect tense portion of the sentence consists of *have* (in one of its three forms) followed by *been* (the past participle form of *be*). *Been* plays a double role. In addition to being the past participle verb form required to form the perfect tense, *been* is at the same time the helping verb *be* required to form the progressive tense. For example:

I <u>have</u> **been** <u>working</u> in the garden all morning.

In this present perfect progressive sentence, we can see that *been* is linked with the verb in front of it (*have*) to form the perfect tense, and it is linked with the verb following it (*working*) to form the progressive tense. We might imagine the two roles of *been* as being played by two separate superimposed verbs, one *been* forming the present perfect tense with *have* and the other *been* forming the progressive tense with *working*:

| have **been** | forms the present perfect portion of the sentence |
| **been** working | forms the progressive portion of the sentence |

There are three different forms that the perfect progressive can take depending on the form that the verb *have* takes: present, past, or future. Here is an example of each:

Present perfect progressive	They **have** been protesting against the new taxes.
Past perfect progressive	They **had** been protesting against the new taxes.
Future perfect progressive	They **will have** been protesting against the new taxes.

EXERCISE

13·1

Each of the following items contains a grammatically correct sentence in one of the three forms of the perfect progressive. Underline all of the verbs that make up the perfect progressive tense and identify which type of perfect progressive tense it is: present perfect progressive, past perfect progressive, or future perfect progressive. The first sentence is done as an example.

She has been introducing all the speakers at the main sessions.

ANSWER: She <u>has been introducing</u> all the speakers at the main sessions.
present perfect progressive

1. He had been scoring nearly half of the team's goals.

2. The painters will have been stripping off all the old paint.

3. They had been washing all the dishes by hand during the power outage.

4. I have been smelling gasoline for days.

5. She will have been studying English since she was in elementary school.

6. Fortunately, I had been keeping a good record of all our building expenses.

7. The wild pigs had been reproducing at a rapid rate.

8. Apparently, they have been posing as reporters.

9. She will have been administering the fund for more than 20 years.

10. The doctor has been prescribing an antifungal drug for me.

The perfect progressive tenses, as with the other progressive tenses, cannot be used with stative verbs. Here are examples for the three perfect progressive tenses using the stative verbs *own, like, understand,* and *sound*:

Present perfect progressive
X Roberta has been owning several sailing boats.
X I have always been liking working in the garden.
X The children have all been understanding what to do in case of fire.
X The idea of a fall vacation has always been sounding like fun.

Past perfect progressive
X Roberta had been owning several sailing boats.
X I had always been liking working in the garden.
X The children had all been understanding what to do in case of fire.
X The idea of a fall vacation had always been sounding like fun.

Future perfect progressive
X Roberta will have been owning several sailing boats.
X I will have always been liking working in the garden.
X The children will have all been understanding what to do in case of fire.
X The idea of a fall vacation will have always been sounding like fun.

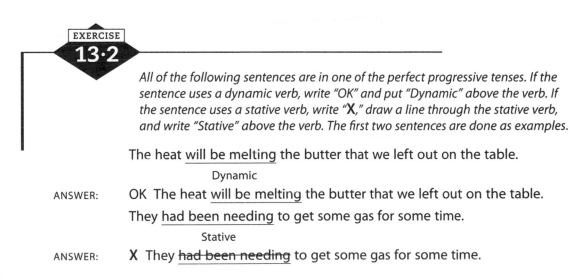

EXERCISE
13·2

All of the following sentences are in one of the perfect progressive tenses. If the sentence uses a dynamic verb, write "OK" and put "Dynamic" above the verb. If the sentence uses a stative verb, write "X," draw a line through the stative verb, and write "Stative" above the verb. The first two sentences are done as examples.

The heat will be melting the butter that we left out on the table.

Dynamic
ANSWER: OK The heat will be melting the butter that we left out on the table.

They had been needing to get some gas for some time.

Stative
ANSWER: **X** They had been needing to get some gas for some time.

1. They <u>have been waiting</u> for a final decision for months.

2. Their decision to get married <u>will have been pleasing</u> to both families.

3. My uncle <u>will have been fishing</u> every day this summer.

4. They were warned that they <u>had been exceeding</u> their budget.

5. He <u>had been recognizing</u> some old friends.

6. I'm afraid that I <u>have been lacking</u> enough money to do it.

7. They <u>have</u> certainly <u>been putting</u> up with a lot lately.

8. Henry <u>had been loving</u> pistachio ice cream ever since he was a child.

9. My old suits <u>had been fitting</u> me again after I had lost all that weight.

10. The government <u>had been exerting</u> a lot of pressure on them to reform.

We will now turn to a detailed examination of the three types of perfect progressive tenses.

Present perfect progressive

The present perfect progressive consists of a present tense form of the helping verb *have* (*has* or *have*) followed by *been* and the main verb in the present participle form (*–ing*). Here are some examples:

> I <u>have been thinking</u> about what you said.
> They <u>have been working</u> on this project for weeks now.
> She <u>has been exhibiting</u> her work in galleries all over the world.
> The head office <u>has</u> really <u>been interfering</u> with our day-to-day operations lately.
> It <u>has been snowing</u> for hours.

The basic function of the present perfect progressive tense is to describe an action or condition that began in the past and has continued in an unbroken manner up to the present time and may continue on into the future; for example:

> Their family <u>has been making</u> wine for five generations.

This definition of the present perfect progressive is virtually the same as the definition of the present perfect tense, and, indeed, with verbs that describe ongoing action, the two tenses can be quite similar in meaning; for example:

Present perfect progressive	The kids <u>have been watching</u> TV all afternoon.
Present perfect	The kids <u>have watched</u> TV all afternoon.

There is, however, something of a difference in emphasis between the two sentences. The present perfect progressive sentence emphasizes the ongoing duration of the TV watching more than does the present perfect sentence.

We can see a real difference between the two tenses quite clearly with most action verbs; for example:

Present perfect progressive	I <u>have been repairing</u> the gear shift on my bike.
Present perfect	I <u>have repaired</u> the gear shift on my bike.

The present perfect progressive sentence describes a work still in progress, while in the present perfect sentence, the job has already been completed. In general, present perfect progressive senses always place a strong emphasis on a process being carried out over time. Present perfect sentences, on the other hand, may or may not imply action in process.

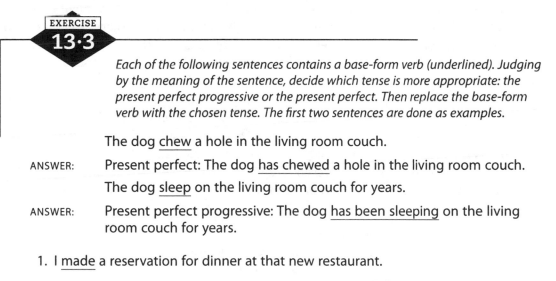

EXERCISE
13·3

Each of the following sentences contains a base-form verb (underlined). Judging by the meaning of the sentence, decide which tense is more appropriate: the present perfect progressive or the present perfect. Then replace the base-form verb with the chosen tense. The first two sentences are done as examples.

The dog <u>chew</u> a hole in the living room couch.

ANSWER: Present perfect: The dog <u>has chewed</u> a hole in the living room couch.

The dog <u>sleep</u> on the living room couch for years.

ANSWER: Present perfect progressive: The dog <u>has been sleeping</u> on the living room couch for years.

1. I <u>made</u> a reservation for dinner at that new restaurant.

2. Grandfather <u>tell</u> that story ever since I was a child.

3. Jackson <u>injured</u> his leg again.

4. The dean <u>recommend</u> her for promotion.

5. Beginning with the Industrial Revolution, the climate steadily <u>warm</u>.

6. The reception <u>be</u> canceled because of the storm.

7. My cousin <u>restore</u> old cars as long as I have known him.

8. The company <u>start</u> a new internship program you might be interested in.

9. Remind me who he is. I <u>forgot</u> his name.

10. It seems as though it <u>rain</u> forever.

The present perfect progressive tense also resembles its other parent, the present progressive. For example, compare the following two sentences:

Present perfect progressive	We <u>have been remodeling</u> our kitchen.
Present progressive	We <u>are remodeling</u> our kitchen.

At first glance, there does not seem to be any real difference between the two tenses. Both sentences describe an action (remodeling the kitchen) that is taking place over a span of present time.

The difference is in how the two tenses treat the meaning of "present time." For the present progressive, "present time" is nothing more or less than the present moment of time; it is an endless "now." The present moment of time is dimensionless: there is no earlier or later. There is no starting the remodeling process in the past; there is no movement across time to the completion of the remodeling project. The present progressive treats time as an indivisible, unitary block.

The present perfect progressive treats time in a different manner. It emphasizes that the action of the verb continues over a span of time up to the present moment.

A particularly striking demonstration of the "timeless" nature of the present progressive tense is the fact that we cannot use adverbs of time that imply duration for the simple reason that there is no duration in present progressive tense sentences. Look what happens when we attempt to add an adverbial of duration (in italics) to our example sentence:

X We <u>are remodeling</u> our kitchen *for the past two weeks*.
X We <u>are remodeling</u> our kitchen *recently*.
X We <u>are remodeling</u> our kitchen *ever since the tree fell on it*.
X We <u>are remodeling</u> our kitchen *since last week*.

These same adverbials of duration are perfectly grammatical with our example present perfect progressive sentence:

We <u>have been remodeling</u> our kitchen *for the past two weeks*.
We <u>have been remodeling</u> our kitchen *recently*.
We <u>have been remodeling</u> our kitchen *ever since the tree fell on it*.
We <u>have been remodeling</u> our kitchen *since last week*.

Past perfect progressive

The past perfect progressive tense consists of *had* (the past tense form of *have*) followed by *been* and the main verb in its present participle form (*–ing*). Here are some examples:

> During that time, I had been working in real estate sales.
> The painters had been stripping the old paint off the walls.
> The truck had been going too fast and lost control on a curve.
> The price of gold had been going up at a steady rate for months.
> The Johnsons had been watering their lawn too heavily.

The past perfect progressive is used to emphasize the continuous nature of an action or event that occurred during a past period of time. There is usually an implication that the past action does not continue beyond that period of time. There can even be an implied contrast between "then" and "now." For example:

> The city had been disposing of its trash by simply burying it.

The use of the past perfect progressive in this sentence strongly implies that the city is no longer disposing of its trash in that manner.

The distinction between the past perfect progressive and past perfect is similar to the distinction between the present perfect progressive and present perfect: the past perfect progressive tense emphasizes the continuous nature of the past action or event. For example, compare the following two sentences:

Past perfect progressive	We had been getting up pretty late.
Past perfect	We had gotten up pretty late.

The past perfect progressive sentence describes a pattern of past activity. The past perfect sentence describes a single past act.

With verbs that describe a continuous action, the two tenses are similar in meaning; for example:

Past perfect progressive	It had been raining all that week.
Past perfect	It had rained all that week.

The only real difference is in emphasis: the past perfect progressive sentence stresses the ongoing, continuous nature of the rain. The past perfect sentence is more neutral: it is simply stating a fact about the weather.

Each of the following sentences contains a base-form verb (underlined). Judging by the meaning of the sentence, decide which tense is more appropriate: the past perfect progressive or the past perfect. Then replace the base-form verb with the chosen tense. The first two sentences are done as examples.

The team <u>play</u> very well until the star player was injured.

ANSWER: Past perfect progressive: The team <u>had been playing</u> very well until the star player was injured.

Someone <u>unlock</u> the pasture gate and the animals got out.

ANSWER: Past perfect: Someone <u>had unlocked</u> the pasture gate and the animals got out.

1. Bobbie <u>scrape</u> his knee playing in the park yesterday.

_____

2. The company <u>accumulate</u> a lot of debt over the past few years.

_____

3. We gave them some toys their parents <u>have</u> when they were children.

_____

4. The crowd <u>swell</u> all afternoon.

_____

5. My knee <u>hurt</u> ever since I was in that automobile accident last winter.

_____

6. They <u>lose</u> control of the fire ever since the winds started blowing.

_____

7. Demand for CDs <u>decrease</u> steadily for the previous 10 years.

_____

8. The explosion totally <u>disrupt</u> the peace negotiations.

_____

9. The dust <u>hang</u> in the air for days.

_____

10. The medication finally <u>clear</u> up the skin rash.

_____

The differences between the past perfect progressive and the past perfect are similar to the differences in the corresponding present tense forms. For example, compare the following sentences:

Past perfect progressive	We <u>had been avoiding</u> the issue.
Past progressive	We <u>were avoiding</u> the issue.

The past perfect progressive sentence spans a period of past time. The past progressive makes a "timeless" factual statement about what happened. We can readily see the difference if we add an adverbial of duration:

Past perfect progressive	We <u>had been avoiding</u> the issue *for some time.*
Past progressive	X We <u>were avoiding</u> the issue *for some time.*

Past progressive sentences cannot be used with adverbials of duration.

Future perfect progressive

The future perfect progressive tense consists of the future form of the verb *have* (*will have*) followed by the past participle *been* and the main verb in the progressive form (*–ing*). Here are some examples:

The opera <u>will have been going</u> on for four hours.
They <u>will have been talking</u> all night.
Thomas <u>will have been missing</u> his parents.
The water line <u>will have been leaking</u> for weeks.

There are two different uses of the future perfect progressive tense: (1) emphasize the duration of an ongoing activity or event and (2) predict actions, attitudes, or events.

Emphasize the duration of an ongoing activity or event

We use the future perfect tense to stress the continuous, unbroken span of time over which an activity or event has been going on, from some past time up to the present moment or to sometime in the near future. The emphasis on duration is so strong that the sentence must contain an adverbial of duration. Here are some examples with the adverbial of duration in italics:

They will have been dating *for nearly a year now.*
We will have been working on this project *for months.*
The International Space Station will have been orbiting the earth *for 13 years.*

If the adverbial of duration is omitted, these examples become incomplete:

X They will have been dating.
X We will have been working on this project.
X The International Space Station will have been orbiting the earth.

The differences between the future perfect progressive and the other two compound future tenses, the future perfect and the future progressive, are in line with the differences we have seen with the other two perfect progressive tenses. For example, compare the following sentences:

Future perfect progressive	They will have been living in Chicago for a year.
Future perfect	They will have lived in Chicago for a year.
Future progressive	They will be living in Chicago for a year.

The future perfect progressive and the future perfect tenses are very much alike. The main difference is that the future perfect progressive tense emphasizes the continuous duration of their stay in Chicago, while the future perfect tense is simply stating a fact.

The future progressive has a totally different meaning from the two future perfect tenses. The future progressive sentence is a statement of their intentions to live in Chicago for a year in the future.

Predict actions, attitudes, or events

The other type of future perfect progressive is used to make a prediction or express a conjecture about what someone or something is doing. (You may recall from Chapter 4 that one of the main functions of *will* is to make predictions.) This use of the future perfect progressive does not require the use of an adverbial of duration. Here are some examples:

We should go in—my parents will have been looking for us.
The defenders will have been strengthening the walls.
All of our cheese will have been melting in this heat.
The competition will not have been expecting our new plan.

Each of the following sentences contains a grammatical sentence in the future perfect progressive tense. Decide which best describes the use of the future perfect progressive tense. Does it (1) comment on the duration of an ongoing activity or event or (2) predict actions, attitudes, or events? If you select the former, write "(1) Duration." If you select the latter, write "(2) Prediction." The first two sentences are done as examples. (Hint: see if there is an adverbial of duration.)

The staff will have been assisting other customers.

ANSWER: (2) Prediction

They will have been driving for nearly an hour by now.

ANSWER: (1) Duration

1. The kids will have been playing football all afternoon.

   _____

2. They will have been wondering what happened to us.

   _____

3. My father will have been working for nearly 40 years.

   _____

4. The company will have been seeking feedback from its suppliers.

   _____

5. We will have been waiting to see a doctor for nearly an hour now.

   _____

6. Everyone will have been getting ready for the big party.

   _____

7. The water will have been flooding through the town for a week.

   _____

8. The candidates will have been buying up TV advertising slots.

   _____

9. They <u>will have been breathing</u> a sigh of relief at the outcome.

   _____

10. I <u>will have been living</u> here for two years this September.

   _____

Answer key

1 Introduction to stative and dynamic verbs

1·1
1. Present tense: I <u>count</u> to 10.   **X**
   Present progressive tense: I <u>am counting</u> to 10.   OK
   Count is a dynamic verb.

2. Present tense: He <u>hates</u> having to repeat himself.   OK
   Present progressive tense: He <u>is hating</u> having to repeat himself.   **X**
   Hate is a stative verb.

3. Present tense: We all <u>hear</u> what we want to hear.   OK
   Present progressive tense: We all <u>are hearing</u> what we want to hear.   **X**
   Hear is a stative verb.

4. Present tense: We <u>want</u> to leave after work as soon as we can.   OK
   Present progressive tense: We <u>are wanting</u> to leave after work as soon as we can.   **X**
   Want is a stative verb.

5. Present tense: The company <u>expands</u> its product line.   **X**
   Present progressive tense: The company <u>is expanding</u> its product line.   OK
   Expand is a dynamic verb.

6. Present tense: I <u>make</u> a reservation for our trip next week.   **X**
   Present progressive tense: I <u>am making</u> a reservation for our trip next week.   OK
   Make is a dynamic verb.

7. Present tense: Their stock portfolio <u>consists</u> largely of bonds and conservative stocks.   OK
   Present progressive tense: Their stock portfolio <u>is consisting largely of bonds and conservative stocks.</u>   **X**
   Consist is a stative verb.

8. Present tense: The publisher <u>reviews</u> her latest book.   **X**
   Present progressive tense: The publisher <u>is reviewing</u> her latest book.   OK
   Review is a dynamic verb.

9. Present tense: John <u>accepts</u> that he is going to have to relocate.   OK
   Present progressive tense: John <u>is accepting</u> that he is going to have to relocate.   **X**
   Accept is a stative verb.

10. Present tense: I <u>know</u> the answer.   OK

   Present progressive tense: I <u>am knowing</u> the answer.   **X**

   Know is a stative verb.

1.2 1. 1: Cognition and emotion   2. 5: Linking verbs with the meaning of appearance and sense perception   3. 3: Ownership and possession   4. 4: Measurement   5. 2: Obligation, necessity, and desire   6. 5: Linking verbs with the meaning of appearance and sense perception   7. 3: Ownership and possession   8. 5: Linking verbs with the meaning of appearance and sense perception   9. 4: Measurement   10. 1: Cognition and emotion

1.3 1. Stative: Nature <u>abhors</u> a vacuum. Category 1: Cognition and emotion

   2. Stative: I <u>suppose</u> that the concert is at 8:00. Category 1: Cognition and emotion

   3. Both verbs are dynamic: John <u>is filling</u> the car with gas while we <u>are getting</u> ready to go.

   4. Stative: Everyone <u>recognizes</u> the need to keep our costs down. Category 1: Cognition and emotion

   5. Dynamic: They <u>are visiting</u> her parents in Detroit this weekend.

   6. Stative: He <u>deserves</u> better treatment than that! Category 2: Obligation, necessity, and desire

   7. Stative: She <u>belongs</u> to a book club that meets once a month. Category 3: Ownership and possession

   8. Dynamic: We <u>are selling</u> what we can't take with us when we move.

   9. Stative: This key <u>fits</u> the door to the garage. Category 4: Measurement

   10. Dynamic: Senator Blather <u>is announcing</u> his support for the trade agreement today.

1.4 1. Dynamic: The saw <u>is getting</u> too hot to operate.

   2. Stative: His idea <u>sounds</u> pretty good to me.

   3. Dynamic: The weather <u>is turning</u> bitterly cold with the wind and cloud cover.

   4. Stative: The pizza <u>looks</u> done.

   5. Stative: I <u>am</u> ready to go whenever you are.

   6. Dynamic: I <u>am becoming</u> more and more optimistic about Aunt Mary's recovery.

   7. Stative: The cloth <u>feels</u> too smooth to be wool.

   8. Stative: His cooking <u>tastes</u> terrible.

   9. Dynamic: The company <u>is becoming</u> a highly successful operation.

   10. Stative: Uh-oh, the vegetables <u>smell</u> burned.

2   The present tense

2.1 1. I can't see you. The light (shine) in my eyes. **is shining**

   The light (shine) against the paintings on the wall. **shines**

   2. The kids (play) in the living room. **are playing**

   The kids (play) indoors when it rains. **play**

3. The company (publish) my first novel. **is publishing**

   The company (publish) works by new authors. **publishes**

4. Bad news always (spread) faster than good news. **spreads**

   The news (spread) all over town. **is spreading**

5. We (gain) weight as we get older. **gain**

   We (gain) weight on this trip. **are gaining**

6. The board (make) the final decision on hiring. **makes**

   The board (make) a bad mistake. **is making**

7. Conflicts about immigration always (divide) communities. **divide**

   The conflict on immigration (divide) the community into factions. **is dividing**

8. The garage always (check) the oil. **checks**

   The mechanic (check) the oil now. **is checking**

9. John (smile) whenever he thinks about what you said. **smiles**

   John (smile) at what you just said. **is smiling**

10. We (walk) every chance we get. **walk**

    We (walk) to the park. Want to come along? **are walking**

2.2   1. Not OK   2. OK   3. Not OK   4. OK   5. Not OK   6. Not OK   7. OK   8. OK
    9. Not OK   10. OK   11. OK   12. Not OK   13. OK   14. Not OK   15. OK

2.3   1. OK habitual   2. OK assertion   3. Not OK   4. OK assertion   5. OK habitual
    6. Not OK   7. Not OK   8. OK habitual (also assertion)   9. Not OK   10. OK assertion

2.4   1. (1) making assertions   2. (3) commenting on present-time actions   3. (1) making
assertions   4. (1) making assertions   5. (3) commenting on present-time actions
6. (2) describing habits   7. (2) describing habits   8. (1) making assertions   9. (1) making
assertions   10. (2) describing habits   11. (3) commenting on present-time actions
12. (1) making assertions   13. (2) describing habits   14. (1) making assertions
15. (1) making assertions

2.5   1. OK   2. Not OK   3. OK   4. Not OK   5. Not OK   6. OK   7. Not OK   8. OK
    9. OK   10. OK

2.6   1. If I see him, I will say hello.

2. Until they save some more money, they will have trouble paying for it.

3. We definitely will accept if they offer us the job.

4. As soon I get home, I will start dinner.

5. We will watch a movie after we finish eating.

6. Once I get my check, I will look for a new apartment.

7. The game still will be played, even if it rains.

8. We will go ahead as planned, even though there are some objections.

9. Unless there is a problem, we will meet you in Denver tomorrow.

10. I will try to visit them next time I go to Phoenix.

1. (6) 2. (5) 3. (4) 4. (5) 5. (1) 6. (1) 7. (2) 8. (7) 9. (3) 10. (1)
11. (6) 12. (2) 13. (3) 14. (7) 15. (4)

3 The past tense

3.1 1. If I were you, I <u>would</u> watch what I <u>ate</u>.

2. If I were you, I <u>would</u> talk only about what I <u>knew</u>.

3. If I were you, I <u>would</u> remind them what they <u>agreed</u> to pay.

4. If I were you, I <u>would</u> be worried about where I <u>parked</u> my car.

5. If I were you, I <u>would</u> start working only when I <u>had</u> enough light to see what I <u>was</u> doing.

3.2 1. What <u>did</u> you think about it?

2. <u>Would</u> you join us for lunch?

3. <u>Could</u> you stop by my office before you leave?

4. <u>Would</u> you be free this evening?

5. <u>Might</u> I make an alternative proposal?

4 The future tense

4.1 1. Prediction 2. Prediction 3. Intention 4. Intention 5. Prediction 6. Intention
7. Prediction 8. Intention 9. Prediction 10. Intention

4.2 1. Everyone <u>stays</u> with friends until the water recedes. Not OK

2. They <u>move</u> out of the apartment at the end of the month. OK

3. I <u>wax</u> the car as soon as the water dries. Not OK

4. We <u>help</u> the public radio fund-raising program Saturday from noon till 4:00. OK

5. Loretta <u>presents</u> the keynote at this year's conference. OK

6. They <u>sell</u> their house as soon as they get a reasonable offer. Not OK

7. The course <u>covers</u> that material in the last week. OK

8. Because of global warming, some insurance companies <u>raise</u> their flood insurance rates next year. Not OK

9. The contractor <u>lays</u> the carpet as soon as he can get the pad installed. Not OK

10. I <u>teach</u> that class next semester. OK

4.3 1. Immediate future action 2. Scheduled or fixed future event 3. Normal expectations
4. New information 5. Immediate future action 6. Scheduled or fixed future event
7. Scheduled or fixed future event 8. Normal expectations 9. Immediate future actions
10. New information

4.4 1. Careful, you <u>are about to sit</u> in a wet chair.

2. The tournament <u>begins</u> this Saturday.

3. I <u>am going to need</u> to rent a car. (Note: <u>am needing</u> is ungrammatical because *need* is a stative verb.)

4. I will turn the lights off when I leave the building.

5. We are about to replace the countertops in the kitchen.

6. They will launch a search for the overdue hikers.

7. The news comes on at 10:00 tonight.

8. The storm is about to hit the coast with heavy rains.

9. The aides will handle all the registration details.

10. He is trying/is going to try a totally new approach.

5 Introduction to the perfect tenses

5.1 1. had checked past perfect   2. has delayed present perfect   3. will have closed future perfect   4. had gone past perfect   5. have started present perfect   6. had gotten past perfect   7. have maintained present perfect   8. will have finished future perfect   9. had anticipated past perfect   10. will have armed future perfect

5.2 1. I have asked them to provide more information.

2. Surely the lake will have frozen by now.

3. We had told them about what they said.

4. They will have cleared customs by now.

5. The court has ruled on many similar cases over the years.

6. Before they moved in, they had repainted the entire apartment.

7. They will have invited more people than they have space for.

8. Fortunately, we had adjusted the insurance before the accident happened.

9. Surely, he has retired by now.

10. His announcement will have attracted a lot of attention.

6 The present perfect tense

6.1 1. Continuously ongoing state (stative)   2. Intermittent action (dynamic)   3. Continuously ongoing state (stative)   4. Intermittent action (dynamic)   5. Intermittent action (dynamic)   6. Continuously ongoing state (stative)   7. Intermittent action (dynamic)   8. Continuously ongoing state (stative)   9. Intermittent action (dynamic)   10. Intermittent action (dynamic)

6.2 1. Noncontinuous   2. Continuous   3. Continuous   4. Noncontinuous   5. Noncontinuous   6. Noncontinuous   7. Continuous   8. Continuous   9. Noncontinuous   10. Continuous

6.3 1. Emphatic   2. Neutral   3. Emphatic   4. Emphatic   5. Neutral   6. Emphatic   7. Neutral   8. Emphatic   9. Neutral   10. Emphatic

6.4 1. Emphatic: The senator has refused to retract his statement.

Neutral: The senator refused to retract his statement.

2. Emphatic: A big tree has fallen in the backyard.

Neutral: A big tree fell in the backyard.

3. Emphatic: A reporter <u>has revealed</u> the source of the money.

   Neutral: A reporter <u>revealed</u> the source of the money.

4. Emphatic: They <u>have told</u> me what happened.

   Neutral: They <u>told</u> me what happened.

5. Emphatic: I <u>have turned</u> down the offer.

   Neutral: I <u>turned</u> down the offer.

6. Emphatic: We <u>have bought</u> a new car.

   Neutral: We <u>bought</u> a new car.

7. Emphatic: I <u>have found</u> my car keys.

   Neutral: I <u>found</u> my car keys.

8. Emphatic: The CEO <u>has seen</u> the new sales figures.

   Neutral: The CEO <u>saw</u> the new sales figures.

9. Emphatic: Our flight <u>has been</u> canceled.

   Neutral: Our flight <u>was</u> canceled.

10. Emphatic: The game <u>has ended</u> in a tie.

    Neutral: The game <u>ended</u> in a tie.

6.5 1. Neutral expectation 2. Affirmative expectation 3. Affirmative expectation 4. Neutral expectation 5. Affirmative expectation 6. Neutral expectation 7. Neutral expectation 8. Affirmative expectation 9. Affirmative expectation 10. Neutral expectation

6.6 1. Affirmative expectation: <u>Has</u> the Coast Guard <u>warned</u> boaters about the storm?

   Neutral: <u>Did</u> the Coast Guard <u>warn</u> boaters about the storm?

2. Affirmative expectation: <u>Has</u> the paint <u>dried</u>?

   Neutral: <u>Did</u> the paint <u>dry</u>?

3. Affirmative expectation: <u>Has</u> the committee <u>adopted</u> the proposal?

   Neutral: <u>Did</u> the committee <u>adopt</u> the proposal?

4. Affirmative expectation: <u>Has</u> he <u>bought</u> the tickets?

   Neutral: <u>Did</u> he <u>buy</u> the tickets?

5. Affirmative expectation: <u>Has</u> the garage <u>checked</u> the battery?

   Neutral: <u>Did</u> the garage <u>check</u> the battery?

6. Affirmative expectation: <u>Have</u> you <u>stayed</u> there before?

   Neutral: <u>Did</u> you <u>stay</u> there before?

7. Affirmative expectation: <u>Has</u> she <u>kept</u> the receipts?

   Neutral: <u>Did</u> she <u>keep</u> the receipts?

8. Affirmative expectation: Have they <u>responded</u> to our offer?

   Neutral: <u>Did</u> they <u>respond</u> to our offer?

9. Affirmative expectation: <u>Have</u> you <u>gotten</u> enough to eat?
   Neutral: <u>Did</u> you <u>get</u> enough to eat?

10. Affirmative expectation: <u>Have</u> they <u>started</u> to work?
    Neutral: <u>Did</u> they <u>start</u> to work?

7 The past perfect tense

7.1

1. We revised the estimates that we <u>had made</u> earlier.
   more recent past-time event   older past-time event

2. He went into the hospital after his temperature <u>had reached</u> 103 degrees.
   more recent past-time event   older past-time event

3. They <u>had patented</u> the device before they put it on the market.
   older past-time event   more recent past-time event

4. I tried to get tickets, but they <u>had</u> already <u>sold</u> out.
   more recent past-time event   older past-time event

5. We fell into bed utterly exhausted as soon as we <u>had eaten</u>.
   more recent past-time event   older past-time event

6. The sun came out for the first time in days after the storm <u>had</u> finally <u>passed</u>.
   more recent past-time event   older past-time event

7. I knew the answer as soon as she <u>had asked</u> the question.
   more recent past-time event   older past-time event

8. I <u>had picked</u> up a cold when I was traveling.
   older past-time event   more recent past-time event

9. We <u>had lived</u> there some time before we met them.
   older past-time event   more recent past-time event

10. The bakery stopped making the cake that everyone <u>had liked</u> so much.
    more recent past-time event   older past-time event

7.2

1. Before we started driving, we <u>had adjusted</u> the car seats.
2. Before everyone finished eating, the waiter <u>had started</u> clearing the dishes.
3. By the time we cut the cake, the ice cream <u>had</u> already <u>melted</u>.
4. When we first moved in, the house <u>had been</u> empty for years.
5. Before I noticed the dirty glasses, we <u>had</u> already <u>finished</u> setting the table.
6. Before the position was approved, he <u>had advertised</u> the job opening.
7. Long before we got on the road, the sun <u>had risen</u>.
8. Before the soldiers arrived, the rebels <u>had</u> already <u>abandoned</u> the fort.
9. By the time we got our tents set up, the rain <u>had stopped</u>.
10. Even before I reached the door, I <u>had heard</u> the loud music.

7.3
1. Normal order: We <u>had taped</u> all the windows and doors before we <u>started</u> painting.
   Inverted: Before we <u>started</u> painting, we <u>had taped</u> all the windows and doors.
2. Normal order: John <u>had</u> already <u>swum</u> competitively before he <u>went</u> to college.
   Inverted: Before he <u>went</u> to college, John <u>had</u> already <u>swum</u> competitively.
3. Normal order: Everyone <u>had put</u> on protective headgear before they <u>went</u> bicycle riding.
   Inverted: Before they <u>went</u> bicycle riding, everyone <u>had put</u> on protective headgear.
4. Normal order: I <u>had skipped</u> lunch because I <u>had</u> an important conference call at noon.
   Inverted: Because I <u>had</u> an important conference call at noon, I <u>had skipped</u> lunch.
5. Normal order: The lawyers <u>had</u> totally <u>revised</u> their strategy before court <u>reconvened</u> after lunch.
   Inverted: Before court <u>reconvened</u> after lunch, the lawyers <u>had</u> totally <u>revised</u> their strategy.
6. Normal order: The cook <u>had rubbed</u> the roast with herbs before he <u>put</u> it in the oven.
   Inverted: Before he <u>put</u> it in the oven, the cook <u>had rubbed</u> the roast with herbs.
7. Normal order: He <u>had hesitated</u> noticeably before he <u>answered</u> the question.
   Inverted: Before he <u>answered</u> the question, he <u>had hesitated</u> noticeably.
8. Normal order: They <u>had drained</u> a lot of water out of the reservoir before the heavy rains <u>came</u>.
   Inverted: Before the heavy rains <u>came</u>, they <u>had drained</u> a lot of water out of the reservoir.
9. Normal order: The company <u>had analyzed</u> the proposal carefully before they <u>invested</u> money in it.
   Inverted: Before they <u>invested</u> money in it, the company <u>had analyzed</u> the proposal carefully.
10. Normal order: They <u>had gotten</u> extra car insurance as soon as their son <u>was</u> old enough to drive.
    Inverted: As soon as their son <u>was</u> old enough to drive, they <u>had gotten</u> extra car insurance.

7.4
1. As soon as the plane <u>had landed</u>, I called them on my cell phone.
2. Even before he <u>had finished</u> asking me the question, I knew the answer.
3. Even before we <u>had found</u> our seats, our team scored.
4. After the sun <u>had come</u> out, we hung the clothes on the line.
5. After we <u>had passed</u> the qualifying exam, we could declare a thesis topic.
6. Even before we'd <u>had</u> a chance to talk about it, I had to come up with a plan.
7. After we <u>had reboarded</u> the bus, we looked for better seats.
8. After the Civil War <u>had ended</u>, General Lee became a college president.
9. After they <u>had repaired</u> it, it functioned much better.
10. After we <u>had sat</u> on the tarmac for an hour, the plane finally took off.

7.5
1. Normal order: They <u>were</u> eligible to play professional football when their class <u>had graduated</u> from college.
   Inverted: When their class <u>had graduated</u> from college, they <u>were</u> eligible to play professional football.

2. Normal order: The airlines <u>instituted</u> a new policy after there <u>had been</u> a near collision on the tarmac.

   Inverted: After there <u>had been</u> a near collision on the tarmac, the airlines <u>instituted</u> a new policy.

3. Normal order: He <u>was</u> arrested after he <u>had lied</u> to the grand jury under oath.

   Inverted: After he <u>had lied</u> to the grand jury under oath, he <u>was</u> arrested.

4. Normal order: Ralph <u>quit</u> his job and moved to Florida after he <u>had won</u> the lottery.

   Inverted: After he <u>had won</u> the lottery, Ralph <u>quit</u> his job and moved to Florida.

5. Normal order: The cloth <u>shrunk</u> badly after it <u>had gotten</u> wet.

   Inverted: After it <u>had gotten</u> wet, the cloth <u>shrunk</u> badly.

6. Normal order: The protesters <u>were</u> arrested after they <u>had disrupted</u> a city council meeting.

   Inverted: After the protestors <u>had disrupted</u> a city council meeting, they <u>were</u> arrested.

7. Normal order: The witness <u>was</u> excused from testifying after she <u>had invoked</u> her right against self-incrimination.

   Inverted: After the witness <u>had invoked</u> her right against self-incrimination, she <u>was</u> excused from testifying.

8. Normal order: Someone <u>called</u> the fire department after the residents <u>had been</u> alerted by the smell of smoke.

   Inverted: After the residents <u>had been</u> alerted by the smell of smoke, someone <u>called</u> the fire department.

9. Normal order: The meetings <u>were</u> better attended after they <u>had started</u> serving refreshments.

   Inverted: After they <u>had started</u> serving refreshments, the meetings <u>were</u> better attended.

10. Normal order: The dog <u>chewed</u> up all the furniture after they <u>had left</u> for work that morning.

    Inverted: After they <u>had left</u> for work that morning, the dog <u>chewed</u> up all the furniture.

8   The future perfect tense

8.1
1. Completed: The two companies <u>will have merged</u> by the end of the fiscal year.
2. Happening: I think that they <u>will make</u> me an offer soon.
3. Completed: They <u>will have traced</u> the source of the leak in a few hours.
4. Happening: The carpets <u>will fade</u> quickly if they are not protected from the sun.
5. Completed: Surely any message they sent <u>will have reached</u> us by now.
6. Completed: Hurry, or they <u>will have sold</u> all the good seats by the time we get our orders in.
7. Happening: The doctor <u>will prescribe</u> a different medication after seeing what happened.
8. Completed: Her heirs <u>will have gained</u> control of their estate when they turned 18.
9. Completed: The chair <u>will have cut</u> off discussion after two hours.
10. Completed: The police <u>will have informed</u> him of his rights the moment he was arrested.

9   Introduction to the progressive tenses

9.1
1. Our company <u>is sponsoring</u> a number of charity auctions. **Present progressive**
2. We <u>were</u> just <u>admiring</u> your garden. **Past progressive**
3. Our pets <u>will be going</u> to the vet for their annual shots. **Future progressive**
4. I <u>am translating</u> some technical manuals into Spanish. **Present progressive**
5. The kids <u>will be staying</u> overnight at a friend's house. **Future progressive**
6. <u>Am</u> I <u>interrupting</u> anything? **Present progressive**
7. They <u>will be completing</u> their training in June. **Future progressive**
8. I <u>was falling</u> asleep at my desk so I took a little walk to wake up. **Past progressive**
9. I don't know why they <u>are blaming</u> me for what happened. **Present progressive**
10. Remember, they <u>will be relying</u> on you. **Future progressive**

9.2
1. You <u>will be wasting</u> your time if you do that.
2. I <u>am making</u> some coffee; would you like some?
3. The polls <u>were leaning</u> toward the incumbent candidate.
4. I <u>will be teaching</u> part-time next year.
5. The heat <u>was killing</u> all of our shade plants.
6. Their flight <u>will be arriving</u> at 9:45.
7. They <u>are referring</u> the whole matter to their legal department.
8. I thought that they <u>were dealing</u> with the situation very well.
9. We <u>will be discussing</u> that issue at our next meeting.
10. His doctor <u>is treating</u> the infection with a new antibiotic.

10   The present progressive tense

10.1
1. The sausages <u>weigh</u> two pounds. **Stative**
   The butcher <u>weighs</u> the sausages. **Dynamic**
   Present progressive: **X** The sausages <u>are weighing</u> two pounds.
   Present progressive: The butcher <u>is weighing</u> the sausages.
2. College graduates <u>pile up</u> a lot of debt. **Dynamic**
   College graduates <u>owe</u> a lot of money. **Stative**
   Present progressive: College graduates <u>are piling</u> up a lot of debt.
   Present progressive: **X** College graduates <u>are owing</u> a lot of money.
3. Bill <u>has</u> a broken toe. **Stative**
   Bill <u>has</u> some friends over to celebrate his promotion. **Dynamic**
   Present progressive: **X** Bill <u>is having</u> a broken toe.
   Present progressive: Bill <u>is having</u> some friends over to celebrate his promotion.

4. The children <u>appear</u> to be ready to go. **Stative**

   The situation <u>changes</u> by the minute. **Dynamic**

   Present progressive: **X** The children <u>are appearing</u> to be ready to go.

   Present progressive: The situation <u>is changing</u> by the minute.

5. The kids always <u>turn</u> their bedroom into a playground. **Dynamic**

   The kids' bedroom <u>resembles</u> the scene of a natural disaster. **Stative**

   Present progressive: The kids <u>are</u> always <u>turning</u> their bedroom into a playground.

   Present progressive: **X** The kids' bedroom <u>is resembling</u> the scene of a natural disaster.

6. Her new hairstyle <u>suits</u> her very well. **Stative**

   Her new hairstyle <u>takes</u> a lot of time to maintain. **Dynamic**

   Present progressive: **X** Her new hairstyle <u>is suiting</u> her very well.

   Present progressive: Her new hairstyle <u>is taking</u> a lot of time to maintain.

7. Everyone <u>tells</u> me to be careful. **Dynamic**

   Everyone <u>needs</u> to be careful. **Stative**

   Present progressive: Everyone <u>is telling</u> me to be careful.

   Present progressive: **X** Everyone <u>is needing</u> to be careful.

8. The public <u>doubts</u> what the congressman is claiming. **Stative**

   The public <u>agrees</u> with what the congressman is claiming. **Dynamic**

   Present progressive: **X** The public <u>is doubting</u> what the congressman is claiming.

   Present progressive: The public <u>is agreeing</u> with what the congressman is claiming.

9. A big payment <u>comes</u> due at the end of the month. **Dynamic**

   A big problem <u>exists</u> in our cash flow. **Stative**

   Present progressive: A big payment <u>is coming</u> due at the end of the month.

   Present progressive: **X** A big problem <u>is existing</u> in our cash flow.

10. The students <u>discussed</u> how to thank you. **Dynamic**

    The students <u>appreciate</u> all that you have done for them. **Stative**

    Present progressive: The students <u>are discussing</u> how to thank you.

    Present progressive: **X** The students <u>are appreciating</u> all that you have done for them.

10.2   1. The chest <u>contains</u> extra blankets and pillows **whenever it gets cold. Stative**

   We <u>take</u> out extra blankets and pillows **whenever it gets cold. Dynamic**

   Present progressive: **X** The chest <u>is containing</u> extra blankets and pillows **whenever it gets cold.**

   Present progressive: We <u>are taking</u> out extra blankets and pillows **whenever it gets cold.**

2. I <u>resolved</u> the issue **in a minute. Dynamic**

   Everyone <u>recognizes</u> the issue **in a minute. Stative**

   Present progressive: I <u>am resolving</u> the issue **in a minute.**

   Present progressive: **X** Everyone <u>is recognizing</u> the issue **in a minute.**

3. We <u>track</u> the paths of protons **when we are in the lab. Dynamic**

   Atoms <u>consist</u> of protons **when we are in the lab. Stative**

   Present progressive: We <u>are tracking</u> the paths of protons **when we are in the lab.**

   Present progressive: **X** Atoms <u>are consisting</u> of protons **when we are in the lab.**

4. They <u>seem</u> to be reliable **all the time. Stative**

   We <u>check</u> on their reliability **all the time. Dynamic**

   Present progressive: **X** They <u>are seeming</u> to be reliable **all the time.**

   Present progressive: We <u>are checking</u> on their reliability **all the time.**

5. He <u>finds</u> out what the answer is **on Wednesday. Dynamic**

   He <u>understands</u> what the answer is **on Wednesday. Stative**

   Present progressive: He <u>is finding</u> out what the answer is **on Wednesday.**

   Present progressive: **X** He <u>is understanding</u> what the answer is **on Wednesday.**

6. The new shoes <u>fit</u> well **every weekend. Stative**

   I <u>wear</u> the new shoes **every weekend. Dynamic**

   Present progressive: **X** The new shoes <u>are fitting</u> well **every weekend.**

   Present progressive: I <u>am wearing</u> the new shoes **every weekend.**

7. We <u>buy</u> a new car **next week. Dynamic**

   A new car <u>costs</u> more than we can afford **next week. Stative**

   Present progressive: We <u>are buying</u> a new car **next week.**

   Present progressive: **X** A new car <u>is costing</u> more than we can afford **next week.**

8. The children <u>love</u> their new school **in the fall. Stative**

   The children <u>enter</u> their new school **in the fall. Dynamic**

   Present progressive: **X** The children <u>are loving</u> their new school **in the fall.**

   Present progressive: The children <u>are entering</u> their new school **in the fall.**

9. Their new apartment <u>looks</u> like their old place **when they move in. Stative**

   They <u>plan</u> to remodel their new apartment **when they move in. Dynamic**

   Present progressive: **X** Their new apartment <u>is looking</u> like their old place **when they move in.**

   Present progressive: They <u>are planning</u> to remodel their new apartment **when they move in.**

10. Everyone <u>helps</u> to rearrange the layout of our office **every Monday morning. Dynamic**

    Everyone <u>dislikes</u> the layout of our office **every Monday morning. Stative**

    Present progressive: Everyone <u>is helping</u> to rearrange the layout of our office **every Monday morning.**

    Present progressive: **X** Everyone <u>is disliking</u> the layout of our office **every Monday morning.**

10.3 1. The baby **is** hungry all the time.   **X**

2. Fortunately, we **have** a laptop at our disposal.   **X**

3. I am <u>supervising</u> a new construction project.   OK

4. The estimate **includes** all taxes and fees.   **X**

5. The kids <u>are mowing</u> the backyard this afternoon.   OK

6. I **hate** the fact that we are having so much trouble.   **X**

7. I don't think it <u>is harming</u> anyone.   OK

8. The ceremony <u>is beginning</u> at 4 p.m.   OK

9. They **all like** the company's new logo.   **X**

10. The heavy rain <u>is ruining</u> everyone's gardens.   OK

10.4
1. The babysitter **is warming** the kids' dinner in the oven.

2. The kids **want** to watch TV until bedtime.

3. Their approval **means** a lot to us.

4. I told the waiter that we **are celebrating** a birthday.

5. George **knows** where the restaurant is.

6. The children **are quarreling** again.

7. We **are soaking** all of our dirty hiking clothes in the washing machine.

8. The purse **belongs** to that young lady over there.

9. The tire **seems** a little flat to me.

10. The flowers in the garden **are blooming**.

10.5
1. **X**   We <s>are hearing</s> the results of the test soon. **Stative**

2. **X**   By Friday, you <s>are needing</s> to give the animals food and fresh water. **Stative**

3. **X**   Getting an upgrade <s>is depending</s> on how much it costs. **Stative**

4. OK   The company is <u>launching</u> its new product line in the fall. **Dynamic**

5. OK   He is <u>undergoing</u> surgery tomorrow morning. **Dynamic**

6. OK   I am <u>buying</u> a ticket as soon as I know my dates. **Dynamic**

7. OK   Mr. Green is <u>retiring</u> at the end of the school year. **Dynamic**

8. OK   My cousins are <u>trying</u> to hike the entire north rim of the Grand Canyon this summer. **Dynamic**

9. **X**   They <s>are recognizing</s> the hotel when they get there. **Stative**

10. **X**   They <s>are</s> certainly <s>appreciating</s> anything you can do for them. **Stative**

10.6
1. Intention   2. Intention   3. Prediction   4. Prediction   5. Intention   6. Intention
7. Intention   8. Intention   9. Intention   10. Prediction

10.7
1. She <u>is going to be</u> on the executive committee starting next week.

2. I <u>am going to have</u> some suggestions tomorrow.

3. Their new apartment <u>is going to seem</u> small after they move all their furniture in.

4. He <u>is going to want</u> to get a new computer if he is going to work from home.

5. Everyone <u>is going to know</u> soon enough.

6. My parents <u>are going to need</u> some help doing the paperwork.

7. His actions <u>are going to seem</u> pretty silly when the results come in.

8. They <u>are going to promise</u> to behave in the future.

9. His grades <u>are going to matter</u> when he applies for a job.

10. Their CEO <u>is going to agree</u> to be interviewed on the record.

10.8

1. He <u>is going to earn</u> a lot of money when he graduates from college.

2. I <u>am going to pass</u> tomorrow's test with flying colors.

3. I think that the court <u>is going to rule</u> in favor of our client.

4. Many investors <u>are going to sit</u> on the sidelines until after the new year.

5. The Dow <u>is going to gain</u> 10 percent by the end of the summer.

10.9

1. (1) action in progress   2. (2) future   3. (4) habitual behavior   4. (3) polite indirectness
5. (4) habitual behavior   6. (2) future   7. (1) action in progress   8. (1) action in progress
9. (2) future   10. (3) polite indirectness or (1) action in progress

11 The past progressive tense

11.1

Stative
1. **X**   We ~~were knowing~~ all along that the job would be difficult.

Dynamic
2. OK   Because of the kitchen repairs, we <u>were eating</u> out a lot.

Dynamic
3. OK   Clearly, all of the politicians <u>were avoiding</u> the issue.

Stative
4. **X**   Frank <u>was</u> always ~~possessing~~ a great sense of humor.

Dynamic
5. OK   The kids <u>were sleeping</u> in a tent in the backyard.

Stative
6. **X**   The orchestra ~~was consisting~~ of a string section and some woodwinds.

Dynamic
7. OK   I <u>was training</u> everyone in the office to use the new accounting software.

Dynamic
8. OK   The government <u>was encouraging</u> everyone to get flu shots.

Stative
9. **X**   After it started raining, the kids ~~were wanting~~ to go home.

Stative
10. **X**   Everyone ~~was needing~~ to take a break because of the heat.

11.2

1. The cold weather <u>threatened</u> to ruin the entire crop.

2. The country <u>was</u> slowly <u>emerging</u> from financial chaos.

3. During the whole time, I <u>was trying</u> to get a word in edgewise.

4. The company rapidly <u>expanded</u> into Asian markets.

5. As it turned out, the police <u>were recording</u> the entire conversation.

6. The heavy truck traffic <u>was damaging</u> the road surfaces.

7. The company <u>represented</u> some of the firms in the industry.

8. All the noise <u>was frightening</u> the children.

9. The kids <u>were swimming</u> at the pool in the community center.

10. Their lawyer <u>advised</u> them not to say anything about what happened.

11.3 1. I was listening to the radio <u>on the way to work</u>.
Confirmation: <u>On the way to work</u>, I was listening to the radio.

2. Everybody was completely on edge <u>after what happened</u>.
Confirmation: <u>After what happened</u>, everybody was completely on edge.

3. The water was flooding the lower fields <u>after all the heavy rains</u>.
Confirmation: <u>After all the heavy rains</u>, the water was flooding the lower fields.

4. They were performing at schools around the state <u>during the fall</u>.
Confirmation: <u>During the fall</u>, they were performing at schools around the state.

5. The police were still questioning witnesses <u>even after the trial started</u>.
Confirmation: <u>Even after the trial started</u>, the police were still questioning witnesses.

6. The wind was blowing faster than 100 miles an hour <u>during the worst of the storm</u>.
Confirmation: <u>During the worst of the storm</u>, the wind was blowing faster than 100 miles an hour.

7. The manager was interviewing ski instructors <u>over the Thanksgiving break</u>.
Confirmation: <u>Over the Thanksgiving break</u>, the manager was interviewing ski instructors.

8. She was working on her master's degree <u>then</u>.
Confirmation: <u>Then</u> she was working on her master's degree.

9. I was just quitting for the night <u>when the alarm sounded</u>.
Confirmation: <u>When the alarm sounded</u>, I was just quitting for the night.

10. Things were looking pretty bad for our candidate <u>before we got the new poll results</u>.
Confirmation: <u>Before we got the new poll results</u>, things were looking pretty bad for our candidate.

11.4 1. Step 1: I <u>was reading</u> a book on my Kindle
Step 2: I <u>was reading</u> a book on my Kindle while everyone else relaxed by the pool.
Step 3: While everyone else relaxed by the pool, I <u>was reading</u> a book on my Kindle.

2. Step 1: When he <u>was undergoing</u> surgery
Step 2: My father suffered a minor stroke when he <u>was undergoing</u> surgery.
Step 3: When he <u>was undergoing</u> surgery, my father suffered a minor stoke.

3. Step 1: The troops <u>were storing</u> ammunition

   Step 2: The troops <u>were storing</u> ammunition when the big explosion happened.

   Step 3: When the big explosion happened, the troops <u>were storing</u> ammunition.

4. Step 1: They <u>were shutting</u> the door

   Step 2: They <u>were shutting</u> the door after the horse was stolen.

   Step 3: After the horse was stolen, they <u>were shutting</u> the door.

5. Step 1: The campers <u>were packing</u> up all their gear

   Step 2: The campers <u>were packing</u> up all their gear when the storm finally broke.

   Step 3: When the storm finally broke, the campers <u>were packing</u> up all their gear.

6. Step 1: While you <u>were talking</u> on the phone

   Step 2: I got all the dishes done while you <u>were talking</u> on the phone.

   Step 3: While you <u>were talking</u> on the phone, I got all the dishes done.

7. Step 1: The fund <u>was investing</u> in Swiss francs

   Step 2: The fund <u>was investing</u> in Swiss francs whenever the dollar was overvalued.

   Step 3: Whenever the dollar was overvalued, the fund <u>was investing</u> in Swiss francs.

8. Step 1: Every time they <u>were doing</u> their homework

   Step 2: We would make the kids give us their cell phones every time they <u>were doing</u> their homework.

   Step 3: Every time they <u>were doing</u> their homework, we would make the kids give us their cell phones.

9. Step 1: The birds <u>were building</u> nests

   Step 2: The birds <u>were building</u> nests whenever they could find a protected place.

   Step 3: Whenever they could find a protected place, the birds <u>were building</u> nests.

10. Step 1: When we <u>were flying</u> in or out of Newark

    Step 2: Our flights were always late when we <u>were flying</u> in or out of Newark.

    Step 3: When we <u>were flying</u> in or out of Newark, our flights were always late.

11.5   1. 3. Habitual actions   2. 4. Failed plans or actions   3. 1. Polite questions and requests
4. 4. Failed plans or actions   5. 6. Disclaiming previous plans or information
6. 2. Tentative suggestions   7. 1. Polite questions and requests   8. 3. Habitual actions
9. 5. Reported informal conversation   10. 2. Tentative suggestions

12   The future progressive tense

12.1   1. **X**   Stative
I <s>will be seeing</s> about it and let you know what I find out.

2. OK   Dynamic
The electrician <u>will be rewiring</u> the kitchen on Monday.

3. **X**   Stative
Their children <s>will be looking</s> just like them.

4. **X**   Stative
     They ~~will not be minding~~ it if we park in their driveway.

5. OK   Dynamic
     The committee will be counting votes tomorrow.

6. **X**   Stative
     The team ~~will be deserving~~ its reputation if they can win today.

7. OK   Dynamic
     The kids will be playing on the swings all afternoon.

8. **X**   Stative
     The dinner ~~will not be including~~ dessert or beverage.

9. OK   Dynamic
     The company will be expanding its online information system.

10. OK   Dynamic
     Ruth will be playing tennis this afternoon with some of her friends.

12.2

1. The principal will be judging the spelling competition at 1 p.m.
Confirmation: At 1 p.m. the principal will be judging the spelling competition.

2. They will be living in Spain until the end of the summer.
Confirmation: Until the end of the summer, they will be living in Spain.

3. We will be continuing the discussion after everyone finishes dinner.
Confirmation: After everyone finishes dinner, we will be continuing the discussion.

4. We will be closing down the beach house after Labor Day.
Confirmation: After Labor Day, we will be closing down the beach house.

5. The sales staff will be showing the apartment as soon as it is vacant.
Confirmation: As soon as it is vacant, the sales staff will be showing the apartment.

6. Department heads will be meeting with the CFO every Monday morning.
Confirmation: Every Monday morning, department heads will be meeting with the CFO.

7. They will be expecting us to begin discussions the minute we get off the plane.
Confirmation: The minute we get off the plane, they will be expecting us to begin discussions.

8. I will be teaching Accounting 101 in the winter quarter.
Confirmation: In the winter quarter, I will be teaching Accounting 101.

9. They will be getting married after she graduates.
Confirmation: After she graduates, they will be getting married.

10. Maintenance will be replacing all the old carpets over the holidays.
Confirmation: Over the holidays, maintenance will be replacing all the old carpets.

12.3

1. Everyone will be rushing to get their taxes in before the April 15 deadline.

2. This last payment will fulfill the terms of the contract.

3. Everyone will be checking their roofs for damage as soon as this terrible wind lets up.

4. The governor <u>will announce</u> the winners of the state awards at the banquet.

5. On the first day of school all the kids <u>will be clinging</u> to their parents.

6. Henry <u>will be editing</u> the white paper before we send it out for review.

7. Everyone <u>will notice</u> that Pat is gone.

8. They <u>will be fishing</u> until it gets too dark to bait their hooks.

9. I <u>will grab</u> a bite at the cafeteria before I go to the meeting.

10. All the rivers <u>will be overflowing</u> their banks after all this rain.

12.4   1. 2. Imagining how someone else feels or thinks   2. 4. Ironic imaginary future
3. 2. Imagining how someone else feels or thinks   4. 3. Indirect invitation or request
5. 1. Planned or expected future event   6. 2. Imagining how someone else feels or thinks
7. 1. Planned or expected future event   8. 3. Indirect invitation or request   9. 1. Planned or
expected future event   10. 4. Ironic imaginary future

13   The perfect progressive tenses

13.1   1. He <u>had been scoring</u> nearly half of the team's goals.
   Past perfect progressive

2. The painters <u>will have been stripping</u> off all the old paint.
   Future perfect progressive

3. They <u>had been washing</u> all the dishes by hand during the power outage.
   Past perfect progressive

4. I <u>have been smelling</u> gasoline for days.
   Present perfect progressive

5. She <u>will have been studying</u> English since she was in elementary school.
   Future perfect progressive

6. Fortunately, I <u>had been keeping</u> a good record of all our building expenses.
   Past perfect progressive

7. The wild pigs <u>had been reproducing</u> at a rapid rate.
   Past perfect progressive

8. Apparently, they <u>have been posing</u> as reporters.
   Present perfect progressive

9. She <u>will have been administering</u> the fund for more than 20 years.
   Future perfect progressive

10. The doctor <u>has been prescribing</u> an antifungal drug for me.
   Present perfect progressive

Dynamic
13.2   1. OK   They <u>have been waiting</u> for a final decision for months.

Stative
2. **X**   Their decision to get married ~~will have been pleasing~~ to both families.

Dynamic
3. OK   My uncle will have been fishing every day this summer.

Dynamic
4. OK   They were warned that they had been exceeding their budget.

Stative
5. **X**   He ~~had been recognizing~~ some old friends.

Stative
6. **X**   I'm afraid that I ~~have been lacking~~ enough money to do it.

Dynamic
7. OK   They have certainly been putting up with a lot lately.

Stative
8. **X**   Henry ~~had been loving~~ pistachio ice cream ever since he was a child.

Stative
9. **X**   My old suits ~~had been fitting~~ me again after I had lost all that weight.

Dynamic
10. OK   The government had been exerting a lot of pressure on them to reform.

13.3
1. Present perfect: I have made a reservation for dinner at that new restaurant.

2. Present perfect progressive: Grandfather has been telling that story ever since I was a child.

3. Present perfect: Jackson has injured his leg again.

4. Present perfect: The dean has recommended her for promotion.

5. Present perfect progressive: Beginning with the Industrial Revolution, the climate has been steadily warming.

6. Present prefect: The reception has been canceled because of the storm.

7. Present perfect progressive: My cousin has been restoring old cars as long as I have known him.

8. Present perfect: The company has started a new internship program you might be interested in.

9. Present perfect: Remind me who he is. I have forgotten his name.

10. Present perfect progressive: It seems as though it has been raining forever.

13.4
1. Past perfect: Bobbie had scraped his knee playing in the park yesterday.

2. Past perfect progressive: The company had been accumulating a lot of debt over the past few years.

3. Past perfect: We gave them some toys their parents had had when they were children.

4. Past perfect progressive: The crowd had been swelling all afternoon.

5. Past perfect: My knee had hurt ever since I was in that automobile accident last winter.

6. Past perfect progressive: They had been losing control of the fire ever since the winds started blowing.

7. Past perfect progressive: Demand for CDs <u>had been decreasing</u> steadily for the previous 10 years.

8. Past perfect: The explosion <u>had</u> totally <u>disrupted</u> the peace negotiations.

9. Past perfect progressive: The dust <u>had been hanging</u> in the air for days.

10. Past perfect: The medication <u>had</u> finally <u>cleared</u> up the skin rash.

13.5   1. (1) Duration   2. (2) Prediction   3. (1) Duration   4. (2) Prediction   5. (1) Duration
6. (2) Prediction   7. (1) Duration   8. (2) Prediction   9. (2) Prediction   10. (1) Duration

About the Author

Mark Lester (Spokane, Washington) is an experienced grammarian, ESL expert, and emeritus college professor. He was the founding chair of the ESL department at the University of Hawaii, which is considered one of the best ESL programs in the United States. He is the author of more than a dozen books, including *A Commonsense Guide to Grammar and Usage* (with Larry Beason), now in its sixth edition, and the widely used college textbook *Grammar and Usage in the Classroom*. For McGraw-Hill, Dr. Lester has authored *Practice Makes Perfect: Advanced English Grammar for ESL Learners*; *McGraw-Hill's Essential ESL Grammar*; *English Grammar Drills*; *The McGraw-Hill Handbook of English Grammar and Usage* (with Larry Beason); and *The Big Book of English Verbs* and *McGraw-Hill's Essential English Irregular Verbs* (with Daniel Franklin and Terry Yokota). Dr. Lester is Eastern Washington University professor emeritus of English and former department chair. He obtained his BA in philosophy and English literature at Pomona College and his PhD in English linguistics from UC–Berkeley. He also holds an MBA from the University of Hawaii.